GETTING THE COUNT RIGHT

GETTING THE COUNT RIGHT

UNDERSTANDING INVENTORY ACCURACY

Greg Schooneveldt

Getting the Count Right: Understanding Inventory Accuracy
Author: Gregory Paul Schooneveldt
First published 2010

RGIS
2000 E. Taylor Road
Auburn Hills, MI 48326, USA

Edited by Averil Lewis
Index by Max McMaster
Cover and text design by Chameleon Print Design
Printed in Australia by BookPal

National Library of Australia Cataloguing-in-Publication entry

Schooneveldt, Gregory Paul.
Getting the count right : understanding inventory accuracy
ISBN: 9781921791444 (pbk.)
Includes index.
Subject: Inventory control.
Dewey number: 658.787

Published by BookPal
www.bookpal.com.au
PO Box 3422
Sunnybank Hills LPO
QLD 4109, AUS

FOREWORD

Few subjects are more critical or more likely to evoke a yawn than 'inventories'. Yet no financial statement, assessment of the condition of an enterprise, pricing, purchase or sale decision can be made without some commercial estimate of the stock of the enterprise.

An inventory is the stock from which crops are planted, products made, and customers satisfied. Farmers have to know how much feed they have, how much fertilizer, how much seed, how much fuel is needed for their farm implements, and so on. Extractors have to know their available equipment, and the approximate amount of remaining resources at a particular site. Manufacturers have to know their available components, sub-assemblies and equipment. Nowhere is an understanding of inventories more crucial than to a retailer. A successful retailer has to understand what is on their shelves, what is on order and the rate at which products are 'moving'.

After five years as CEO of RGIS™ (Retail Grocery Inventory Services), the largest third-party inventory service in the world, I am acutely aware of how little valid research has been done in this area. Greg Schooneveldt's willingness to undertake the rigorous work necessary to advance our understanding of this crucial subject is a real contribution to everyone interested in this field.

When Greg and I first discussed the writing of this book, it was always clear that the principal objective of any inventory is to provide the most accurate representation of the stock possible. But 'inventory accuracy' is a nebulous term, often confused with other concepts like 'precision' and 'different methods of measurement'. Importantly, Greg clearly explains all of these concepts and measures accuracy in a range of controlled settings.

Inventory accuracy comes at a price and the 'perfect' count must consider acceptable error, given the value of the item. Clearly, counting expensive jewelry or life-saving pharmaceuticals justifies a much higher willingness to pay for accuracy than counting cans of soda. Add to this the complexity that in most environments, the count is accurate for only a short time.

Our clients have always demanded accuracy and precision at an economical price. We believe that we deliver this better than anyone else can—including their own employees. In this book, Greg explains the nature of inventory accuracy and precision and the commercial and practical realities that determine them. Unlike a boring inventory, it is a refreshing wake-up call.

Paul Street
CEO
RGIS
Auburn Hills
Michigan USA
March 2010

CONTENTS

PREFACE

Why write a book about inventory accuracy? Ostensibly inventories—recorded lists—are long, specialized and very dull reading. I certainly did not begin my working life interested in them. I grew up in the suburbs of Melbourne, Australia; my parents were post-war Dutch immigrants. I obtained my first degree in psychology at the University of Melbourne and later a PhD in psycho-acoustics at the University of Cambridge, UK. Returning to Australia in 1989, I became increasingly involved in my father-in-law's inventory services business, Lotons. It began with my writing stock count software systems for handheld technology. Later, I became managing director and the business grew throughout Australasia. In 2007 the company and I joined the largest inventory services enterprise in the world, RGIS™. The company has offices in 25 countries, 40,000 employees and performs 400,000 stock counts a year. My current role is President, Asia Pacific.

Over the years I have come to appreciate that the humble, boring and often maligned inventory is absolutely central to our lives and daily existence. Inventories are in fact symbolic representations of all things important to us in our world. Without them the shopping would not be bought, the 'to do' items would be forgotten and everyday enterprises, large and small, could not function.

In recent decades the inventory itself has undergone a revolution, moving from a written list to a digital representation inside the modern computer. Computer systems permit convenient input of inventory data, secure and massive storage capacity and fast access. Importantly, the computerized inventory provides a powerful analytic platform from which enterprises can glean commercial insights into their operations and stock.

Despite so many advances in technology and processes, people still have to physically count stock in order to establish and verify the inventory. The stock count remains a largely manual task. And maintaining an accurate inventory is still not trivial. In an active enterprise in today's world, stock is constantly moving and the inventory must accurately reflect changing stock levels through time.

The definition of inventory accuracy is often not well understood or reliably measured. Furthermore, inventory literature is of little help—it seems polarized between the very scientific and the largely anecdotal. Journal articles tend to be complex and laden with theory and formulae from which it is often difficult to extract practical applications. Alternatively, many inventory accuracy books offer few citations and little analytic rigor to support claims or methods. They may contain helpful anecdotal information but it is often based on unsubstantiated opinion.

Should one ask any enterprise manager rhetorically, 'Do you want an accurate inventory?', they are quick to reply emphatically, 'Of course!'. But when one is more specific and asks, 'How accurate?', and 'How much do you expect to pay for that?', they struggle to answer. High inventory accuracy is achievable, but it costs time and money. This book strives to systematically analyze the nature of the inventory and the stock count process. It defines and measures the process and effort needed to achieve accuracy.

Getting the Count Right is divided into six parts. Part I considers the nature of the inventory, its purpose and history. Parts II and III examine the role of finance and the influence of technology on the inventory and stock count.

Part IV outlines the theory of inventory 'accuracy', distinguishing it from other related but sometimes confused concepts such as 'precision'. Part V separates the stock count process into stages and measures accuracy in each. Lastly, Part VI consolidates these findings, outlining the best stock count practices.

Much of this research was made possible because of the resources of RGIS. A laboratory store was established at the RGIS research facility in Auburn Hills, Michigan. This provided a controlled environment in which stock, people, technology and processes were rigorously tested in pursuit of the best stock count practices that achieve reliable levels of accuracy in commercial periods of time.

While the research is supported by statistical analysis, I have intentionally avoided the unnecessary use of formulae and statistical concepts that may confuse some readers. My emphasis is on explaining complex ideas simply.

This book is intended for those whose work involves the systematic counting of stock and inventory verification, including enterprise managers, accounting auditors, inventory service providers, and those who want a clear explanation of inventory accuracy concepts, measurement and practical methods.

Gregory Paul Schooneveldt
March 2010

LIST OF ILLUSTRATIONS

ACKNOWLEDGMENTS

Any book requires a huge effort. Helping with this project have been several researchers, consultant statisticians and inventory business and stock count managers at RGIS™. These people have assisted to examine the literature, review the technology and complete rigorous analysis on inventory accuracy practices and measurement.

My heartfelt thanks to Blair Cleave, Rebecca Konkolesky and Nick Warren. They provided much valuable data collection, literature research, statistical analysis and lively discussion.

I am grateful to RGIS management, particularly Paul Street, for supporting the idea, and to James Bell, Alan Birck, Xudong Cao, Richard Cauchi, Dave Feidner and Michael O'Connor for invaluable suggestions and reviews.

My special thanks to the publishing team, particularly Averil Lewis for her editing and guidance, as well as Max McMaster, Luke Harris and Carolyn Leslie.

Lastly, thank you to my wife Kathryn and children Conrad and Yvette, for putting up with my absent-mindedness while I worked whenever I could steal a moment.

PART I: CONCEPTS

1: Inventory definition

Most enterprises store and hold in their care some goods or 'stock'. The stock may consist of raw materials, work in progress or finished products. The holding of stock helps the enterprise manage fluctuating supply and demand over time and constitutes part of its financial assets. This is especially true for enterprises in manufacturing, logistics and retail, where good stock control is critical to ensure business profitability and accountability.

The term 'inventory' is used to refer to a list or record of goods or stock. It is derived from the medieval English (1375–1425) 'inventorie' which stems from the early Latin 'inventōrium' and 'inventārium'.[1] While the stock is the physical asset, the inventory is a representation of it at one point in time.

Unfortunately, in modern English the word 'inventory' has three distinct meanings and so is often ambiguous. The noun 'inventory' can mean both a stock record, such as a list, or it can refer to the physical stock itself. 'Inventory' can also be a verb and refer to the act of recording stock. For example, it is quite acceptable to ask: 'Can you inventory the stock?'

Thus there are three different meanings for the same word: the list, the stock and the process. To avoid confusion, in this book a list or record of stock is called an 'inventory'. The term 'stock' is used to refer to physical goods. Lastly, the term 'stock count' is used to indicate the process of counting and recording the stock. In this context 'stock count' also means the same as the British term 'stocktake'.

The organization that holds stock is referred to as an 'enterprise'. The term enterprise was chosen because it is generic, and serves to include any entity that holds stock, such as commercial businesses, private organizations and governments and their departments, including the military.

In this section basic inventory concepts are examined. The purpose and history of the inventory are considered in respect to advances in technology and the nature of people who create and maintain them.

1.1   The written list

Creating inventories is a peculiarly human activity. We tend to record details and form lists of all manner of things. Ostensibly the recording of an inventory converts the representation of the physical object into a convenient symbolic format—the written word. Figure 1.1 presents an inventory of cattle destroyed by wolves in 1824.

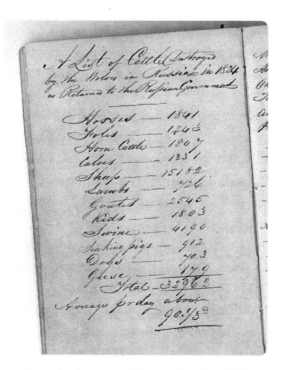

Figure 1.1: List of cattle destroyed by wolves in 1824.

Unlike physical items, the inventory is supremely portable and easily folded in our pocket or stored inside a computer hard drive. It can be stored indefinitely and sent electronically around the world in an instant. Importantly, it reminds us about every detail at a glance, without having to see physically the items of interest.

In an enterprise, the inventory facilitates the monitoring of its stock. The simple inventory provides a description, location, and quantity for each item. It answers basic stock questions like 'what', 'where' and 'how many'? By linking other timely information, such as item pricing and stock movements, the inventory becomes an invaluable management tool that reflects the commercial health and the profitability of the enterprise.

Of course, the fundamental requirement of the inventory is that it is accurate at any point in time. The moment the physical stock changes (due to sales, purchases, transfers or shrinkage) the inventory must be correctly updated. Through time, as movements occur, there is a risk that the inventory and the stock will increasingly mismatch. Only by revisiting the physical stock, and by reconciling and updating each item with the existing inventory, will accuracy be assured. This is the nature of any inventory:

- to be of use it must be accurate and reflect the items that it describes
- the stock count remains the essential tool needed to establish its veracity and accuracy.

1.2 The computer database

The invention of the computer in the late 20th century shifted the enterprise inventory from paper ledgers to electronic databases. The computer database has allowed the efficient storage, retrieval and manipulation of vast inventories over time.

As digital speed and capacity has improved, computer inventory systems have evolved where stock quantities are updated as transactions occur. Computerized inventory systems synthesize stock sales, purchases and transfers constantly. By recording and combining all stock movements they generate a theoretical or 'perpetual' inventory over time.

In theory, if all enterprise transactions are correctly recorded and processed in the computer inventory system, the resulting perpetual inventory should always accurately represent the physical stock.

With improving computer technology the size and complexity of the underlying inventory database has increased. In particular, the development of the ubiquitous barcode and barcode-reading technology provided a reliable and inexpensive means to capture and store stock information like item numbers and locations.

Data fields now commonly included in most inventory databases are item number (sometimes called the stock keeping unit or SKU), manufacturer's barcode, item description (in both long and short versions), location, minimum stock holding and quantity, supplier, department, cost price and retail price. Figure 1.2 illustrates a stock status report generated by a perpetual stock system. It shows sample stock inventory data fields stored in the underlying database.

Stock Status Report

03:31pm

For Month of February in Financial Year
By Department

Code	Description	Dpt	- Sales MTD - $	Qty	Qty OnHand	Latest Cost	Stock Value	B/Ord Qty	B/Ord Value	Days Cover	Stock Turns	YTD ROI	LYR ROI	YTD ASP
1063326	End Connector Pol X Fl 1"	057	8.89	2	-2 8	2.63	-5.25	0	0.00	0	-4.4	0	0	4.09
1706025	Floor Waste Vinyl Base 50M	057	96.82	6	-1	11.96	-11.96	0	0.00	0	-4.4	0	0	16.14
1066726	Flushpipe Wh Mid Level Str	057	28.05	1	-1 /	19.76	-19.76	0	0.00	0	-4.4	0	0	28.05
1063205	Joiner Pol X Pol 1"	057	10.46	2	-2 /2	3.33	-6.66	0	0.00	0	-4.4	0	0	5.14
1700199	Nut & Tail Brass 3/8 Nut X	057	8.18	4	-4	1.02	-4.06	0	0.00	0	-4.4	0	0	2.10
1730781	Plug Chr / Brass 40Mm	057	5.32	1	-1	2.95	-2.95	0	0.00	0	-4.4	0	0	4.96
1063012	Poly Pipe Rural Class B 1"	057	111.10	154.5	-112.5	0.46	-52.14	0	0.00	0	-4.4	0	0	0.76
1063014	Poly Pipe Rural Class B 1-	057	59.23	43	-15	0.71	-10.65	0	0.00	0	-4.4	0	0	1.37
1049042	Pres Pipe Class 9 40Mm-Cut	057	24.00	4.4	-4.4	2.27	-9.97	0	0.00	0	-4.4	0	0	4.42
1080983	Priming Fluid Red 4L	057	33.80	2	-1 0	11.05	-11.05	0	0.00	0	-4.4	0	0	15.86
1700656	Quick Anchor 3/4" Copper B	057	21.41	1	-1	10.70	-10.70	0	0.00	0	-4.4	0	0	21.41
1051402	Service Tube C/P Copper 1/	057	23.96	3	-3	5.57	-16.71	0	0.00	0	-4.4	0	0	7.21
1080961	Solvent Cement Clear 500Ml	057	21.25	5	-4	3.24	-12.96	0	0.00	0	-4.4	0	0	4.00
1046073	S/Water Coupling Slip 90M	057	180.02	40	-10 5	2.00	-20.00	40	80.00	0	-4.4	0	0	3.76
1046003	S/Water Pipe 90Mm-Cut	057	283.97	66.5	-25.73	2.34	-60.14	0	0.00	0	-4.4	0	0	3.84
1046015	S/Water Pipe 300Mm	057	449.54	2	-1	200.35	-200.35	1	200.35	0	-4.4	0	0	199.17
057	TOTAL Dept 057 GENERAL PLUM		2,096.62	446.1			-681.96		423.54		-14.3	-7	4413	

Figure 1.2: Sample computer system inventory report.

Of course, inventory data must be relevant and accurate if it is to be of value. The old adage 'garbage in—garbage out' will apply: if inaccurate data is kept or entered into a computer inventory system, only inaccurate information can be gleaned from it. On the other hand, it is pointless to maintain a high level of inventory detail and accuracy if the cost of doing so brings little or no commercial benefit to the enterprise.

Each inventory data field requires resources to establish, maintain and report. These resources cost time and money to maintain. The maintenance of a perpetual inventory must be justified through enhancing enterprise operations by increasing efficiency, reliability or profitability. The accurate inventory is one tool, among others, that facilitates the sound operation of an enterprise and naturally its benefits must outweigh its cost.

1.3   The visual representation

With improvements in computer technology (faster processors, more memory, better graphics, etc.) inventories have moved beyond written lists and electronic databases to images and visual representations.

Over the last 20 years, computerized merchandising stock systems using computer-aided design software technology have been developed. These provide a number of visual representations of the stock environment. Essentially they generate two- and three-dimensional images of stock and its relative placement in space.

Figure 1.3 illustrates a simple two-dimensional retail store floor plan. The boxes represent the floor space including the gondolas, counters and cash registers, as well as the store room at the back of the store. Each gondola is divided into numbered sections called 'fixtures'.

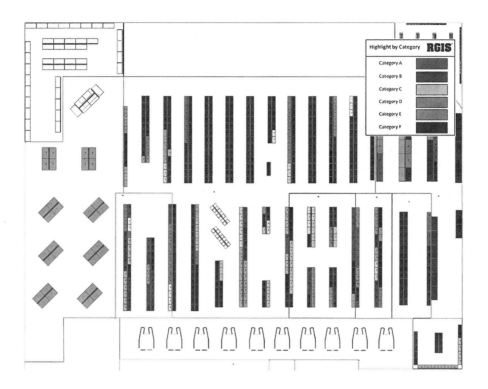

Figure 1.3: Schematic stock floor plan of a large retail store (courtesy of RGIS Storplanner™).

The relationship between the physical stock and its storage space is maintained by the merchandising stock system. Any inventory field linked to this space can be visually displayed on a floor plan. For instance, stock characteristics of interest such as category, shrinkage, sales or profit can be displayed on the floor plan. These relationships can be expressed using 'heat maps' where a range of values for any variable are represented by different colors or shading (see Figure 1.3).

Actual stock placement on each fixture can also be represented by planograms. Planograms are elevation drawings of stock storage units and provide a standing view of the stock. They more clearly illustrate the exact placement and adjacencies of each item of stock. Figure 1.4 illustrates a planogram of a single gondola fixture. Ideally, stock is laid out in its most appealing and efficient order so as to attract sales and maximize the revenue for each unit of retail space.

A graph can present data more clearly than a list of numbers. So too, a floor plan or planogram can display stock–space relationships more clearly than an inventory list. This thinking extends the logical concept that the inventory can be any representation of physical stock in any format.

Figure 1.4: Illustration of a two-fixture planogram (courtesy of RGIS Storplanner™).

1.4   Stock, asset and other inventories

Any list of items is arguably an inventory, although the term is generally reserved for inanimate objects. It is not common to refer to an 'inventory of employees' or an 'inventory of clients', although it is possible.

This book largely focuses on stock inventories. Stock inventories refer to those goods that are a central source of income and activity in manufacturing distribution or retail enterprises. They are the items that the enterprise trades in. There are broadly four types:[2]

- raw materials and consumables used in a production process such as unprocessed items
- work in progress or partially completed products that have had value added but are not yet complete
- finished goods which are ready to be stored, on-sold or delivered
- other quarantined stock which is placed in a special class due to its unique characteristics or circumstances. Examples may include obsolete or damaged items, excess supply, over-runs, prototypes and special orders.

Another type of inventory maintained by many enterprises is an asset register, or asset inventory. Items likely to be included in an asset register may be tangible or intangible. They are those items of value that help an enterprise fulfill its core purpose and goals. Examples include:

- plant and machinery
- office furniture
- electronic equipment
- artwork and memorabilia
- software, including licenses
- building fit-outs, fixtures and improvements
- patents, trademarks and licenses
- service contracts, warranties.

Asset registers have many of the characteristics of stock inventories, including asset number (equivalent to an item number), description, price and location. However, there are many additional fields that can be maintained in an asset register, such as service history, warranty life, operational condition, written-down or depreciated value and so on. Asset registers are discussed more fully in Chapter 8.

1.5 Summary

A representation of stock

In this book the term 'inventory' refers to a list or record of items. Enterprises use the inventory to provide a representation of their stock. The earliest inventories were handwritten, but the development of the computer provided a means to store the inventory in an electronic stock database and the production of other visual formats such as a planogram.

Enterprise inventories

The modern enterprise manages a number of inventories. Examples include the stock count inventory, the perpetual inventory and the asset register. A simple inventory, perhaps generated by a stock count, will describe each item of stock, its location and quantity. By maintaining the inventory in a computer system linked to purchase and sales data, a perpetual inventory can be established and maintained, providing a powerful management tool.

2: Inventory purpose

Stock is sometimes called 'the asset that nobody wants'. It costs money to buy, secure and maintain. However, trading enterprises understand that they need to hold stock in order to:

- avoid the supply chain time lag between stock order, delivery and consumption
- ensure a safe buffer in the event of unexpected changes in stock supply, demand or movement
- enjoy economies of scale such as bulk buying and the sharing of fixed expenses over larger stock holdings.

In short, the purpose of holding stock is to help manage supply and demand within the enterprise.

In order to manage and control the stock the enterprise uses the inventory. Most authors agree on the functions or purposes of the stock inventory.[3] However, each arranges and emphasizes these very differently depending on their interest. The purpose of the stock inventory can be arranged under four categories.

The inventory serves to:

- represent and track the existence of stock, particularly its description, location, cost and quantity
- facilitate the accurate and fast valuation of stock, in order to meet legal and accounting requirements
- enable risk management of stock, minimize stock loss, shrinkage and obsolescence
- optimize stock levels and movement, reduce manufacture and storage costs, and maximize sales and profits.

Each of these purposes is considered in more detail below.

2.1 Stock representation

The first purpose of an inventory is reasonably simple: to provide a representation of physical stock. Access to the inventory provides information about the stock, negating the need to actually see it.

Life without an inventory

Consider an enterprise with lots of stock, but without a meaningful inventory. Each variety or item of stock would be unique, with a different quantity, price and location. Without an independent inventory to refer to, employees would need to remember the stock and form their own mental representation of it. They would each develop individually unique descriptions, locations and prices.

Since their memory would vary in detail and accuracy, asking them to find the correct stock and establish an agreed quantity and price would be virtually impossible. To know that the stock existed, employees would need to find and visit an item location to check its quantity. Furthermore, they could not agree on a quantity for a particular item from one moment to the next without checking, since item quantities would be subject to change without any formal record. Thus an enterprise with stock and without an inventory would suffer from poor accuracy and productivity.

Ideally, the inventory representation is:
- **secure,** being stored in a safe place and maintained only by those with appropriate knowledge and authority
- **standardized,** being in a formal and logical structure that is easily reproducible
- **accessible,** where it can be quickly and easily retrieved, reached, updated and reported
- **portable,** integrated and transferable to other systems, formats and databases
- **timely,** where it reflects the physical stock at a required and defined moment including the present

- **testable,** where its presentation lends itself to verification and reconciliation with the actual stock
- **accurate** and trustworthy, from which informed decisions can be made.

In short, the fundamental role of the inventory is to provide an accessible, accurate, documented description of the stock at a point in time.

2.2 Stock valuation

The second purpose of the inventory is to record an accurate valuation of the stock. The need to 'value' or 'cost' stock is obvious. Stock is an asset, and its worth at any moment in time is of constant concern to any enterprise stakeholder such as a manager, owner or creditor.

A 'valuation' refers to the likely amount of money for which an item can be exchanged. All enterprises are legally obliged to meet minimum accounting standards and to annually report their trading activity, including a valuation of their stock. The inventory provides the means by which stock is recorded and valued.

The notion of value is really an estimate that varies depending on the time, purpose or circumstance for which a stock valuation is required.[4] Perpetual inventories include one or more item price fields that represent different notions of value. Examples include: retail price, different supplier prices, historical purchase price, current price or an average of several prices. Whichever price field is chosen, a total stock valuation is generated by multiplying each item's quantity by its corresponding value and summing for all items.

The specific price field used to determine the item's valuation will change depending on the exact circumstances for which the valuation is required. There are several valuation concepts to consider, given the purpose of the valuation. These are summarized below and are more fully outlined in Chapter 5.

- **Financial value**, which typically uses invoice cost prices for periodical accounting and reporting of commercial accounts.

- **Market value**, which uses current supplier cost prices for the sale of business, where an enterprise is transferred from one owner or entity to another.
- **Reinstatement value**, which uses current supplier cost prices for the purpose of insurance and credit applications.
- **Realizable** or **salvage value**, which uses a discount cost price, in the event of enterprise receivership or insolvency.

2.3   Stock security

The third purpose of the inventory is security. Since stock is a valuable asset, it must be stored securely and monitored in order to identify and reduce theft and damage. All enterprises invest considerable time and effort to reduce risk and protect their stock.

The most common method used to define and measure stock loss is shrinkage. Shrinkage refers to stock that is lost, damaged, stolen or spoiled in the course of business. Its cause may be intentional such as theft by employees, suppliers or customers, or it may result from accidental administrative errors observed in paperwork, receipting, storage, picking or dispatch.

Lost stock reflects lost sales and therefore shrinkage can be considered as 'intended sales income that was not or cannot be realized'.[5] More formally, shrinkage is measured as the difference between the theoretical retail stock value and the actual stock retail value.[6] The theoretical stock value is calculated using the sales and purchase data over a fixed period. It may be aggregated or maintained at an item level using a perpetual inventory system. The actual stock value can be derived using a stock count and valuation at the end of a period.

To illustrate using a simple example: if 120 units of a particular stock item are bought and 100 are then sold at $1.00 each, theoretically there should be 20 left. However, if a stock count revealed say only 19 units, then one item must have been lost or stolen. This difference between the theoretical and the actual stock is called 'shrinkage'.

It is usually expressed as a percentage of retail sales, where, using the example above:

$$\$1 \text{ loss} / \$100 \text{ sales} \times 100 = 1\% \text{ shrinkage}.$$

The stock count inventory helps to measure and identify shrinkage. However, it is difficult for any enterprise to completely eliminate shrinkage. The University of Florida conducts an annual National Retail Security Survey.[7] Under the auspices of the Security Research Project it has studied aspects of workplace crime and deviance, especially in the retail industry. Their annual survey provides empirical data on retail loss prevention, asset protection and security.

The 2007 survey of 134 retailers in the US reporting shrinkage as a percentage of their retail sales was 1.44 per cent.[8] This corresponds to approximately US\$34.8 billion annually in the US alone, a staggering amount. The report states that 'among the major sources of inventory shrinkage, retailers attributed 44% of their company's losses to employee theft, 34% to shoplifting, 15% to administrative error, 4% to vendor fraud and 3% to unknown error'. Other research has observed similar trends. Employee theft is particularly common during tough economic periods.

The variety and causes of shrinkage are subtle and widespread. Consider just one common form of shrinkage—employee theft in a retail enterprise.[9] For brevity, some of the methods used are listed below:

- direct theft of goods or point-of-sale monies
- under-charging customer accomplices
- adjusting transfer and delivery dockets
- under-ringing purchases at the point-of-sale
- fiddling the inventory shrinkage records
- deliberately damaging and reporting damaged goods in order to buy them at an employee discount
- increasing creditors' invoices and keeping the difference
- replacing perfect items with seconds
- fraudulent refunding.

Now consider some of the common administration anomalies that lead to shrinkage:

- paperwork errors, particularly illegible handwriting and incorrect arithmetic
- stock keypunching errors, particularly incorrect item numbers, quantity, store numbers or transaction dates
- recording of the wrong stock units, such as singles instead of cases or boxes
- recording of the wrong prices due to incorrect exchange rates, exclusion of taxes or wrong item prices
- loss of data due to failed back-up and storage procedures.

There are numerous strategies which have evolved to tackle the many sources of shrinkage. The interaction between the cause and prevention of shrinkage is a constant game of cat and mouse. Strategies include:

- regular cyclic and full stock counts
- extensive paperwork with cross-referencing
- computerized inventory and sales systems
- barcode, RFID and other stock marking and labeling systems
- on-site security cages, security tags, sensor systems and alarms
- video and other surveillance systems
- employee education and procedures
- security guards and bag searches.

Left uncontrolled, shrinkage undermines four aspects of the enterprise—stock level, employee morale, customer satisfaction and commercial viability. Simply measured as the valuation difference at an instant in time between a perpetual inventory (derived by recording stock movements) and a stock count inventory (derived by an immediate physical count of all stock), it is a central indicator of enterprise performance. Chapter 5 examines other finance aspects of shrinkage.

2.4   Stock optimization

The final purpose of the inventory is to facilitate the control of the stock level, also known as 'stock optimization'. Ideally, in any enterprise, the stock type, quantity, location and value is monitored and controlled precisely over time. In manufacturing and logistics environments, much emphasis is placed on the physical storage and timely access of the stock in order to minimize stock holding costs, reduce error and maximize profitability. Retailers share these goals, but must also emphasize the actual merchandising of the stock. In particular, they will consider the available space at a store, fixture and shelf level in order to maximize stock appeal and sales.

An accurate inventory in isolation cannot optimize stock, however, it does provide the means of analysis. A study of historical sales, purchases and inventory levels over time will highlight seasonal trends and opportunities to reduce stock holding costs for overstocked items, while maintaining or improving sales on fast moving items. This information can be utilized by both experienced and novice managers alike.

Choosing the right level of purchases to complement sales is a compromise between having too much and too little. Maintaining low stock levels saves enterprises money by reducing stock costs, lowering storage and handling costs and reducing the likelihood of shrinkage, spoilage and obsolescence.

However low stock levels also have some disadvantages. They reduce the benefits of economies of scale; limiting the opportunity to buy in bulk to receive better discounts, or more favorable terms. Low stock levels are likely to require more frequent replenishment, leaving enterprises dependent on the availability and reliability of third party suppliers. They also increase the risk of stock run-outs leading to:

- loss of production targets and deadlines
- loss of sales, orders, customer goodwill and reputation
- unproductive or redundant employees, equipment and resources.

Of course, maintaining high stock levels increases the probability that, given current demand, there will always be stock-on-hand. But this overstocking comes at a price. High stock levels can waste money because they:

- require additional resources, such as warehouse space, to receive, record and store
- increase security and workforce costs needed to prevent theft
- increase the risk of stock perishing by damage or obsolescence
- deplete cash flows, reducing opportunities for alternative money usage.

Competent manufacturer and logistics managers will seek to complete a cost-benefit analysis to determine the correct stock levels over time.[10] External factors to consider are supplier reliability, demand predictability, price fluctuations, bulk purchase discounts and cash flow. Internal factors include the production or manufacture time, logistics such as stock receipting and picking time and storage facility capacity and costs.

Good stock optimization includes the maximizing of the retail space. Retailers pay a premium for smart, appealing, high-traffic space in shopping strips and malls. Each item of stock uses this space and must justify its location and existence through its profit and monetary returns.

Merchandising stock systems are sophisticated computer software programs that generate optimal space, fixture and on-shelf stock recommendations based on business models, forecasts, sales and profit potential. They assist enterprises in considering their inventory in terms of the space used, and the profits and costs this generates.

Stock optimization: a simple case study

A cosmetic manufacturer, using a merchandising stock system, designed a planogram that graphically presented the optimal arrangement of their range of nail polishes for retail customers. The planogram considered historical sales and shrinkage data from a number of the leading retail stores. Photographs for each item were stored in the system. These were visually arranged in any order to maximize their merchandise appeal.

Based on the available information, the best-selling colors were placed at eye height in the order of their base shades. To minimize shrinkage, stock was displayed only on three shelves above waist height. Lockable drawers were placed below to conveniently store reserve stock. The manufacturer ensured that their shelves looked uncluttered and attractive.

The merchandising system generated a planogram report detailing each item number and description in order for each fixture shelf. This was sent to each retail store explaining that this was the recommended stock arrangement to maximize sales.

In the weeks that followed stock counts were completed of the displayed stock and compared to the planogram to determine if stores had indeed arranged the stock as requested. These 'realograms' compared the stock on the shelf with the required planogram and indicated stock placement differences. Sales were also monitored to determine any changes.

In sum, the merchandising stock system provided the means to systematically and conveniently store, manipulate, communicate and test stock placement.

Stock optimization seeks to control costs and improve sales. Examples include ensuring stock levels meet fluctuations in supply and demand and that stock is arranged to minimize shrinkage and enhance the shopping experience. Alternatively, poor stock control can lead to overstocking or stock-outs and lost sales. Stock optimization depends on an accurate inventory in order to monitor and test optimization strategies.

2.5   Summary

The inventory serves four main purposes: the representation, valuation, protection, and the optimization of stock.

Representation
An inventory provides a symbolic representation of the physical stock. It is used to describe, summarize, communicate and analyze the stock over time. Without an accurate inventory the modern stock holding enterprise could not function commercially.

Valuation
An inventory can be used to quickly and easily value stock (where the quantity for each item is multiplied by the price and summed for all items). This is essential for enterprises to meet basic legal and accounting requirements.

Security
Stock is a valuable asset and needs protection, security and monitoring. An inventory can be used to calculate shrinkage (by comparing theoretical stock levels with actual stock levels). This helps the enterprise identify items prone to damage, theft, administration error and loss. It also provides a means to measure the impact of procedures and strategies used to address shrinkage.

Optimization
An inventory can be used to monitor stock and its location. By ensuring optimal stock levels and the most appealing arrangement, stock holding costs and stock run-out may be reduced and sales appeal maximized.

3: Inventory history

3.1 Earliest inventories

In its most common form, an inventory is merely a list of just about anything. For centuries, kings and scholars, amateurs and professionals have recorded items of interest and value in every detail. Some of the earliest known Egyptian writing from around 3400 BCE[11] consisted of small 'inventory tags' made of ivory, bone and stone. These were inscribed with hieroglyphics, attached to jugs and other items and served to 'convey some accounting information' like the object's provenance or its quantity.[12] Such tags were effectively carrying stock inventory information, like the supplier and quantity.[13]

The New York Metropolitan Museum of Art holds on display a clay tablet dated from 1365 to 1330 BCE. The tablet records an 'inventory of gifts' sent by the Mitanni king to celebrate his daughter's wedding to an Egyptian pharaoh. Among the gifts are 'beautiful' and 'swift' horses, a chariot, whips, reins and bridles, many of which were made from gold.

Time and civilization brought other writing systems. The Hebrew, Aramaic and Greek scripts originated from the Phoenician. The Greek alphabet led to Latin and Cyrillic. Aramaic led to Arabic and many of the scripts used in India. Paper was invented by the Chinese about 2000 years ago and by 600 CE it was widely used to record the handwritten word. But the communication of all knowledge was revolutionized when Johann Gutenberg invented the printing press in 1453.

Inventories can be found throughout recorded history. The Bible refers to the census that required Joseph and Mary to return

Figure 3.1: Example of ancient Egyptian hieroglyphic detail.

to Bethlehem.[14] The Domesday Book commissioned by William the Conqueror after he invaded England in 1085 records details of some 13,000 settlements and landowners in the English counties south of Scotland. Also of historical significance are the records kept by royal navies, local clergy and every trader throughout the 16th, 17th and 18th centuries.[15]

3.2   Inventory and accounting

The introduction of formal accounting is often credited to the Franciscan friar Luca Pacioli in 1494.[16] He was the first to describe the principal of double-entry bookkeeping (where for every credit entered into a ledger there must be a debit). Accounting practice remained largely centered around bookkeeping until the industrial revolution in the late 18th century, when the benefits of cost accounting were discovered. Enterprises could calculate the cost of material and labor for each step of manufacturing process before adding a profit margin to ensure commercial viability. Such analyses highlighted the value of stock and the inventory as a means to monitor it.

By the mid-19th century accountants were becoming common in Europe and the US with the establishment of the American Institute of Certified Public Accountants (AICPA) in 1887.[17] However, periodic booms and busts, including the Great Depression, identified the need for better accounting consistency and transparency. The introduction of financial accounting sought to define standards, free from bias, for the reporting to investors, creditors, and other external stakeholders. Inventory stock valuations were needed to support accounting calculations of the cost of goods sold and gross profit.

Today all countries have their own laws and inventory accounting rules, but the practices are merging. In the US, the Generally Accepted Accounting Practices (GAAP) (largely defined by the Financial Accounting Standards Board [FASB] are enforced by the US Securities and Exchange Commission [SEC]). About 100 other countries use the London-based International Financial Reporting Standards [FRC]. These formal accounting principles highlight the efforts being made globally to provide transparent and professional standards and policies.

Periodic and perpetual stock systems

Basic accounting practice requires transactions to be systematically recorded under accounts in ledgers. Traditionally, sales dockets and purchase invoices were recorded periodically by their total monetary value and not at an item level at the time of the transaction. To review and drill into an account balance, filed invoices and sales records for the given period were searched. This was a tedious and time-consuming undertaking.

Since stock was not recorded at an item level, a stock inventory could not be generated from the accounts. Instead, at the end of a selected period a stock count was necessary to provide a remaining stock inventory and valuation. This stock valuation was used to calculate the cost of goods sold and complete the financial accounts for the period.

The development of the perpetual stock system allowed the storage and reporting of all stock transactions at an item level through time. As item transactions were processed by the system, the stock inventory was automatically updated. This inventory could be printed at any point in time, not just available at the end of a period. The introduction of the perpetual stock system was only made possible because of the speed and capacity of the modern computer system.

3.3   Inventory and information technology

In the past 50 years the information technology revolution has made the maintenance of the stock inventory easier. The handwritten inventory in the form of a ledger or stock sheet was replaced by the calculator, which was then replaced by the computer. New technology has improved the methods, speed, detail and accuracy by which the inventory is established and maintained.

The stock sheet inventory

To verify physical stock, a stock count is required from which an inventory is produced. Traditionally, the inventory consisted of handwritten paper stock sheets. Much like a ledger, a printed stock sheet provides rows and columns that facilitate clearer handwriting and prompts the required data. Figure 3.2 shows a simple inventory recorded on a handwritten stock sheet with an item description and quantity.

QTY	NAME	PRICE 200s	250s		QTY	NAME	PRICE 200s	250s	
20	ALBANY	92.77	18.55		20	HALLMARK	92.15	18.43	
20	ALBANY TRIM	81.95	16.39		20	KENT SOFT	92.15	18.43	
					25	"	81.14	16.23	20.29
20	ALPINE	91.85	18.37						
25	ALPINE	81.14	16.23	20.29	25	JOHN PLAYER	77.93	15.59	19.49
					30	" "	73.39	17.61 (240)	2.20
25	ARBATH	74.96	14.99	18.74	20				
20	BENSON-HEDGES	92.15	18.43		20	KOOL	92.15	18.43	
20	" " PLAIN	92.77	18.55						
25	" "	81.14	16.23	20.29	20	LARK	103.29	20.66	
30	BLACK + WHITE	67.21	16.13 (240)	2.02	20	L+M	98.65	19.73	
40	BRANDON	56.59	11.32	2.26	25	LONG BEACH	66.05	13.21	16.51
25	BELMONT	77.93	15.59	19.49	40	"	58.14	11.63	2.33
30	CAMBRIDGE	65.35	14.76 (180)	1.96	20	LUCKY STRIKE	96.79	19.36	
35	"	62.91	13.21 (210)	2.20	20	MARLBORO Imp	90.92	18.18	
20	CAMEL FILTER	99.89	19.98		20	MARLBORO	94.32	18.86	
20	" SOFT	99.89	19.98		20	" GOLD	100.81	20.16	
20	" REGULAR	100.81	20.16		25	"	82.63	16.53	20.66
					30	MARTIN	69.06	16.57 (240)	2.07
20	CAPSTAN	90.61	18.12		20	MORE	107.00	21.40	
20	CARTIER VENDOME	98.65	19.73		25	NOW	78.92	15.78	19.73
20	CHESTERFIELD REG	94.94	18.99		20	MILD SEVEN	97.72	19.54	
20	" KING	100.40	20.08		20	MILD SEVEN INT	120.92	24.18	
25	CLARIDGE	72.24	14.45	18.06					
30	COMMODORE	69.89	16.77 (240)	2.10	30	NELSON	64.32	15.44 (240)	1.93
20	CRAVEN A CORK	93.08	18.42		20	PALL MALL	102.98	20.40	
20	" " REG	92.15	18.43						
25	CRAVEN A	81.89	16.38	20.48	25	PARK DRIVE	80.16	16.03	20.04

Figure 3.2: *Handwritten price and stock count sheet.*

To value the stock, a clerk would apply a cost price for each listed item. In practice, the price of some common items might be recalled from memory, but most required a review of the invoice record. The item cost multiplied by its quantity determined the item's stock value. By summing all item values for each stock sheet and tallying all stock sheets, a completed stock valuation was achieved.

A stock count using stock sheets is effectively an itemized inventory. If the sheets are numbered and include the counter's name and location, they serve as an audit trail and can be reviewed at any time. The resulting stock valuation can then be used for financial reporting.

Unfortunately the summing, costing and valuing of a stock sheet inventory is very laborious and may take weeks. Errors in counting, cost price application, transcription and arithmetic could undermine the accuracy of the inventory at each stage. For retailers, employee hours were consumed on non-core retail activities. If the store was closed during the stock count, valuable sales were lost. Alternatively, if the stock count was completed after hours or on non-trading days, additional wage costs were incurred.

Calculators

The abacus is among the oldest known aid to mental calculation, various forms of which arose in ancient Greece and China, predating the modern numeral system. The device is usually a frame with counting beads or stones and many can still be found in use today in parts of Africa and Asia.

Mechanical calculators originated in the early 16th century. Various mathematicians and inventors, including Leonardo da Vinci, built a range of devices.[18] The late 19th century saw the arrival of calculators which were relatively heavy mechanical devices. However, it was not until the 20th century that such machines were used on a large scale. Electric desktop calculators became common after 1960 and with the development of electronic transistor and silicon micro chips by the 1970s, calculators had shrunk in size, weight and cost. In the 1980s, smaller battery-operated devices with digital displays and soft touch keyboards emerged. These were small and light enough to comfortably hold in one's hand.

Successful enterprises have always used the inventory to review and manage their stock. But the counting and valuing of stock using handwritten stock sheets remained slow, error prone and expensive. This tedium was made worse when the stock count was only used to derive a stock valuation for financial reporting.

Electric calculators were popular among retailers and made the execution of simple stock counts and valuations faster and cheaper.

During calculator stock counts in the 1970s, people worked in pairs. A 'caller' would count all items with the same retail price, calling out the quantity and marked retail as they went. Alongside them, a 'clerk' would keypunch the quantity and retail price into the calculator. The calculator would print the price multiplied by quantity and store a running total. The running total could be printed when required by choosing the sub-total, or printed and cleared by choosing the 'total' key.

Stock was easily separated and counted in departments. The average percentage of profit for each department was multiplied by the total retail stock value to obtain the average stock profit. By deducting the total retail stock value from the average stock profit an estimate of the stock value at cost was achieved. This method was often called a 'financial inventory' because it only consisted of the retail price and quantity summed to provide a total stock value for financial purposes. (Chapter 5 provides a detailed description of profit margin concepts).

Stock counts using calculators were generally faster than those using stock sheets. There was no need for stock item details to be written, cost prices found or manual arithmetic. Small counting teams could be used and the stock valuation could be generated immediately on completion of the count. These savings meant that retailers could verify their stock value more frequently. If stores were performing poorly or the stock valuation was in doubt, a recount was easily conducted. This was particularly helpful for growing 'big box' retailers with fluctuating stock levels and varied product ranges.

Calculator stock counts had a number of disadvantages. Unlike stock sheets, calculator stock counts did not provide a detailed inventory describing each item of stock. Counting errors and anomalies were easily lost in the long data entry sequences of retail and quantity. There was no transparent audit trail of item numbers or descriptions to conveniently review and check. Also, the stock valuations were not based on researched purchase history or current cost prices, but estimated using retail less approximate profit margins.

Handheld computers

Smaller, cheaper and more powerful computers allowed the storage and manipulation of larger and more complex inventories. However, human data entry remained relatively slow, monotonous and prone to keypunch error.

Fortunately, during the 1980s, a range of barcode styles and barcode reading devices was developed. Such automated data entry systems, particularly the printed barcode, served to make item number data entry fast and accurate. Barcode readers were soon integrated with small handheld computers. These portable devices could be placed anywhere near stock, including at the point-of-sale on conveyors or on vehicles (see Chapter 12 for an overview).

Such technology was of immediate interest to enterprises with large and dynamic stock holdings. Manufacturers could mark and identify their products cheaply and easily, while retailers now had a means to capture sales at an item level at the check-out.[19]

During stock counts, instead of a caller and clerk working in pairs, people could work alone. A single 'stock counter' could scan and collect barcode data and then count and store the stock quantity. This was fast and less prone to stock sheet transcription errors.

Over time, computers and other handheld devices revolutionized the stock count and valuation process. The stock count shifted from merely counting and valuing stock using calculators (summing quantity multiplied by price) and returned to collecting a more detailed inventory (recording each item number and quantity).

The stock details were typically processed in a batch, days or even hours after collection. This meant that neatly printed and itemized inventory reports with stock valuations could be generated soon after the stock count. This level of automation was much faster and more accurate than laborious, handwritten and error-prone stock sheets.

3.4 Perpetual stock systems

Smaller, cheaper and more powerful computers allowed the development of sophisticated inventory management software systems such as Retail Point of Sale (POS), Manufacturing Resource Planning (MRP II) and Enterprise Information Systems (EIS).[20]

Such systems maintain a live or 'perpetual' inventory as stock transactions (sales, purchases, transfers and shrinkage) are recorded and processed. This facilitates real-time detailed stock level monitoring and reporting. For instance, perpetual stock systems can automatically re-order stock if levels are below set thresholds. Where in the past it was necessary to check all stock on the shelf before placing an order, today a computer system automatically generates a list of recommended re-orders.[21]

To be of value, however, the perpetual inventory must hold the correct location and quantity for each item. To establish and verify the perpetual inventory a stock count is required. Perpetual stock systems often support both stock sheets and handheld devices for stock counts. While handheld devices can capture and transfer data electronically, as before, stock sheets require data to be manually keypunched, a process which is slower and more error prone.

3.5 Merchandise stock systems

Consider the general store of the 19th century. Stock was allocated where it could most conveniently fit. Dry grocery, grains and the like were stored in timber and metal containers to reduce the infestation of weevils or mice. Some stock was placed in broad areas of convenience; perhaps hardware items in one area, haberdashery in another and clothing in a third. Items were either good or poor sellers. Merchandising consisted of a simple motto: 'Stack 'em high and watch 'em fly'. Little consideration was given to the profit an item would generate according to the space it occupied.

However, traders gradually realized that their placement of stock in a shop could affect sales. Shop windows promote sale stock to passers-by. Supermarket check-outs tempt waiting customers with impulse buys of confectionery and magazines. Gondola ends and display bins showcase promotional areas like weekly specials and discounted items. In addition, many manufacturers provide bonus stock to retailers that display their stock favorably. Leading food and beverage manufacturers have long understood that stock displayed at eye height and with multiple facings improves sales.[22]

Merchandising stock systems evaluate the physical position of stock in a shop. Specifically, they seek to:

- map physical features at a macro level using floor plans and at a micro fixture and shelf level using planograms
- generate heat maps to visually display space and other stock-related variables (such as items sales, profit, shrinkage and categories)
- optimize available fixture space, stock and stock adjacencies using business rules, forecasted demand, and profit potential
- systematically measure and compare alternative space configurations using two- and three-dimensional drawings and images.

Early merchandising stock systems developed in the mid-1980s include Nielsen's Spaceman and Information Resource's Apollo. More recent systems include RGIS' Storplanner™.

Importantly, merchandising stock systems utilize the stock inventory by combining it with other related information and presenting it visually. For a more detailed discussion of these systems refer to Chapter 9.

The history of independent inventory service providers

Traditionally, enterprises conducted their own stock counts using their employees. However, in England in 1846, Benjamin Brogden Orridge started his own enterprise conducting stock counts for others. He was a pharmacist to Queen Victoria and a founder of the Royal Pharmaceutical Society. [23]

With such good connections, he established Orridge Ltd, a 'Business Sales Brokerage' firm to act as an agent for buyers and sellers of pharmacies. He soon realized that buyers and sellers could rarely agree on a commercial value for their stock. They needed an independent 'umpire', or referee, to provide an honest and objective 'appraisement of stock and fixtures'. In 1850 the firm also began providing stock counts for hardware and other retail stores.

The stock count methods used by Orridge remained largely unchanged for over 100 years. A 'caller' would count and call out each item of stock and a 'writer' would write its details onto a stock sheet. On completion of the count the stock sheets were then sent off to an office where the numbers were 'comped' (added up) and discounts applied for obsolete or damaged items. A 'certified valuation' report was then sent to the client indicating the valuation of the stock.[24]

Throughout the world, during the booming economic years following World War 2, many retailers evolved from single store 'Mom and Pop businesses' into multi-store chain operations. Retail management soon noticed that some people were faster and more accurate stock counters than others. Consequently, larger retail groups established their own specialized stock counting teams who would travel from store to store to count inventories.

Some entrepreneurial individuals began providing independent inventory services for retailers. In 1958 a former supermarket manager from Detroit, Thomas J. Nicholson, began RGIS. Initially, stock counts were completed using stock sheets, but as technology improved, RGIS established electric calculator inventories in the 1970s, and later handheld computer inventories in the 1980s.

In other world regions, more service providers emerged. In the 1950s George Loton began providing stocktake services for grocers in Australia and later New Zealand. Washington Inventory Service was established in 1953 and, in 2005, merged with Canada's largest service provider Western Inventory Service (1967) to form 'WIS International'.[25] AJIS in Japan began in 1978 and are today a public company.[26]

Other independent inventory services enterprises are found throughout Europe, Asia and the Americas. By far the largest worldwide inventory service provider is RGIS, with offices in 25 countries and around 400,000 stock counts annually.

3.6   Summary

History

Inventories can be found throughout recorded history. The earliest civilizations created inventories describing things of interest and value. In its most common form, an inventory is merely a list.

Financial applications

The introduction of formal accounting emphasized the need to maintain an accurate stock inventory. The periodic stock count served to generate an inventory and stock valuation to assist in the preparation of annual financial reporting.

Inventory service providers

With increasing demand for accurate stock inventories, throughout the late 20th century independent inventory service providers evolved, conducting stock counts as needed for growing enterprises.

The technology revolution

Early stock counts used stock sheets. Later, calculators and eventually handheld computer devices recorded stock details including the item description, location quantity and price. Computer systems that maintain a perpetual inventory provided a means to itemize and analyze stock.

Perpetual stock systems

Perpetual stock systems support the reporting of stock transactions at the itemized inventory level. This gives the enterprise a much more detailed analysis of stock movements than previously available with manual stock record-keeping.

Merchandising stock systems

Merchandising stock systems present stock visually and can be used to highlight placement of an item relative to shop fixtures and other stock items. This gives the enterprise insight into the distribution of stock within a three-dimensional space.

4: Stock and people

Despite developments in technology and process, inventory accuracy is neither fully automated nor guaranteed. Certainly computer technology has led to improvements in the stock count and perpetual inventories. For instance, the scanning and capture of barcodes has improved the speed and accuracy of the stock count; whereas the automated recording of stock movements has improved the timeliness and detail of the perpetual inventory. But regardless of these enormous advancements, inventory accuracy is still affected by two underpinning factors:
- stock—its characteristics and environment
- people—their ability, motivation and skill.

4.1   The nature of stock

Modern manufacturing and logistics practices have led to the improved packaging of stock and its storage. These developments facilitate inventory accuracy. Historically, merchants used to sell stock by weight and in unmarked packaging and variable units. The imperial system was complex and not well understood among the largely illiterate masses. For instance, the 'baker's dozen' was the medieval practice of providing 13 units for the price of 12, in order to guard the baker against accusations of cheating his customers. Today the packaging and arrangement of stock is much more consistently and formally defined, but there remain issues.

Stock characteristics

Stock characteristics like the item type, container, packaging and weight are all relevant factors that affect inventory accuracy. In modern warehousing, stored stock is usually boxed in its manufacturer's ubiquitous brown cardboard. Some boxes may be clearly labeled but, depending on their source, others may be marked in a foreign language or not marked at all. Without reference to a shelf or item number such stock is difficult to identify.

In the retail sector, manufacturers will adorn their stock with eye-catching color and design, but often telling one variety from another is difficult and at the whim of marketers, whose interests may not take into account the needs of the humble stock counter.

Stock environment

The environment in which the stock is stored also affects inventory accuracy. Consider for a moment two enterprises with the same stock and trading patterns, but stored in different environments.

First, imagine a modern efficient warehouse, well lit and temperature controlled, with the stock easily identifiable, arranged neatly in rows or packed in well-marked boxes. Most stock is stored at normal working heights and any item is stored in only one location with a unit or box quantity of 100 or less.

Alternatively, imagine the same stock in a far more disorganized and onerous environment. There is no stable heating or cooling, the stock is poorly marked, dirty and its identity is unknown or unrecognizable. The same item is in multiple locations and many locations house more than one item. Much of the stock is stored in unmarked boxes with different units in each box. The stock is stored in pallet racking six levels high so a large proportion of it can only be accessed using a forklift or scissor lift.

The characteristics of the stock and its environment will affect people's ability to maintain an inventory that accurately represents it. In the first example the environment is conducive to inventory maintenance. The second example, however, presents numerous physical obstacles that are likely to impede inventory accuracy and make any stock count longer and more prone to error.

4.2   The nature of people

Despite advances in technology and modern manufacturing, packaging and storage, the establishment and maintenance of the inventory is still not fully automated. People are still required to identify, count and verify physical stock and record this detail in the inventory. Inventory management is still a people business, and therefore subject to the limitations of human beings and the physical nature of stock.

Ability

Cognitive psychologists have long recognized that our conscious ability to attend to one thing while ignoring others is limited and this ability fatigues over time. There are only so many jobs that we can do concurrently and for a sustained period. Most stock count processes using a handheld device only require the counter to record the stock location at the start of a section, repeatedly scan or keypunch each item, count and record its quantity and then mark the completed location ticket before continuing to the next location.

This task is ostensibly easy and can be completed all day, subject to modest breaks every few hours. However, if the stock counter is asked to do additional tasks while scanning, counting and keypunching, their accuracy and/or their speed is likely to deteriorate.

Additional tasks might include requiring the counter to separate similar-looking stock, identify obsolete or damaged stock, collect additional fields such as a serial number or retail price, and sort poorly arranged stock. If tasks are added—each increasing the counter's cognitive load—their ability to count and record data accurately will obviously suffer. People's cognitive and physical ability is finite.

Skill: stock counting

A central requirement at any stock count is that people are numerate and can identify and count the physical stock quickly and accurately. In truth, the notion of '"numeracy" is a deeply contested and notoriously slippery concept, and the subject of lively debate by commentators'.[27]

RGIS, among other inventory service providers, test prospective employees to ensure that they have basic numeracy. Figure 4.1 is a sample page of a stock counting aptitude test developed by RGIS. The test requires each applicant to count the number of items in each of 40 spatial illustrations in less than five minutes. The pictures are of typical stock configuration and require basic arithmetic to quickly and reliably count and record the correct quantity.

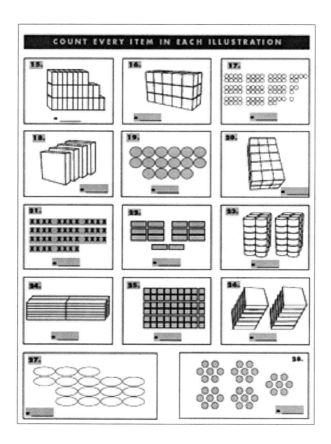

Figure 4.1: Sample stock count numeracy test.

Over several years, more than 18,000 adult Americans have been tested. This includes students, retirees, parents looking for part-time work, and full-time workers seeking to become professional stock counters.

Of those selected for employment the average score was 73% correct (or 29/40). These people were likely to be motivated since they were tested when applying for a job. Now, 73% correct is probably a respectable result, but would an enterprise be content with 27% of inventory error? Probably not. Yet this is the likely counting ability available to every enterprise. Any stock count process needs to be developed with this basic level of counting skill in mind.

Skill: stock identification

It is noteworthy that the RGIS prospective employee test (see Figure 4.1) only required one item type to be counted in each question. Another essential human skill underpinning inventory accuracy is to identify and distinguish similar, yet different items.

Consider a simple example to clarify this point. Figure 4.2 shows a picture of whiteboard marking pens. When an audience is asked to count these pens they instantly call out a quantity of 4. When asked to state how many retail price points there are, they take more time, sometimes argue among themselves and report a range of answers typically from 2 to 4. Finally, when asked to nominate the number of unique item numbers (SKUs) present, they take more time and reply with a range of answers from 1 to 4. Consider their options with even this simple example of pen varieties. They can allocate:

- 4 highlighters with one item number
- 3 Artline manufactured, 1 Expo manufactured
- 2 Artline 577, 1 Artline 500A, 1 Expo
- 1 Artline 577 red, 1 Artline 577 black, 1 Artline 500A and 1 Expo.

Figure 4.2: Stock count of four highlighter pens.

Clearly there are several ways to distinguish the four pens at an item level, but only one will be correct as required by the enterprise or circumstance. If the pens were counted using one item number, when there are in fact four item numbers, four inventory errors are generated.

Stock that looks similar is easily confused and prone to identification error. Often it is a failure to identify the stock correctly that leads to counting errors, rather than merely an inability to count accurately.

Experimental results suggest that people can count, but the accuracy and speed with which they can find and correctly distinguish items varies depending on the stock and level of practice (see Chapter 16).

Motivation

Motivation refers to the drives and reasons that people behave in a certain way. It affects our ability to count quickly and accurately. Stock counting is repetitive and requires high levels of concentration over long periods. This often leads to boredom and fatigue.

People need to earn adequate money to motivate them to work hard. The adage: 'If you pay peanuts you will get monkeys', holds. If the salary is not commercially attractive, the quality of the people will be poor. They will also feel that their work is meaningless, since they are paid so little. This in turn leads to low self-esteem, low work morale and ultimately poor work.

People perform best when they are accountable for the work that they do. In fact it has been shown experimentally that people's behavior will improve simply by the act of measurement alone and not in response to any particular environmental change. In the 1950s Henry Landsberger coined this phenomenon the 'Hawthorne Effect'. He analyzed old experiments from 1924–32 at the Hawthorne Works (a Western Electric-owned manufacturing factory near Chicago). The Hawthorne Works had commissioned a study to see if its employees would become more productive in higher or lower levels of light. Surprisingly, once employees became aware of the study their productivity improved, regardless of the level of the light or other factors.

In general, simply taking an interest or measuring people's behavior can improve it. If their work is not checked or reviewed, there is little reason to try harder. Making employees accountable can also make them feel valued and appreciated. Their work is needed and monitored because of its importance and value to the enterprise.

Good stock count practice provides counters with performance feedback during and after the course of the stock count. The average units counted per hour (APH) indicates relative productivity and can be used to compare counters or performance in similar stock environments. For instance, the APH in a book store where a large proportion of items are barcode-scanned individually may vary from around 600 to 900. By contrast, a supermarket, with an average item quantity of around 10, will have an APH nearer 2000.

In 2002 the United States General Accounting Office (GAO) produced a best-practices guide to achieving an accurate inventory. The GAO studied seven companies with 'leading-edge inventory count process and procedures' to determine the key factors and practices needed to achieve consistent and accurate stock counts.[28]

They observed that in order to motivate and control the stock count process, management must be engaged and accountable. This included establishing performance goals with achievable levels of accuracy that were measured and enforced.

4.3   Summary

Stock
Inventory accuracy is affected by the nature of the stock. Influencing characteristics are its packaging, descriptive labeling, units of storage, barcode or number labeling. Environmental factors are its storage height, accessibility, temperature, visibility, shelf labeling and quantity. Well-prepared stock facilitates accurate inventories.

People
People's ability, skill and motivation affect the degree of speed and accuracy with which they count and record stock. Despite advances in technology and improved stock characteristics and environments, people are still required to identify, count and verify physical stock and record this detail in the inventory. Inventory management is still a people business and subject to the limitations of human nature.

I: Notes

1   *The American Heritage Dictionary of the English Language.* 4th edn: Houghton Mifflin Company, 2004.

2   Kutz, Gregory. *Executive Guide: Best Practice in Achieving Consistent, Accurate Physical Counts of Inventory and Related Property.* Washington: United States General Accounting Office, 2002.

     Brooks, Roger B. and Wilson, Larry W. *Inventory Record Accuracy.* Hoboken, New Jersey: John Wiley & Sons, 2007.

3   Kutz, p. 6.

     Brooks and Wilson.

     Piasecki, David J. *Inventory Accuracy: People Processes and Technology.* Kenosha: OPS Publishing, 2003, p. 5.

4   IVSC. *International Valuation Standards 8th Edition.* London: International Valuation Standards Committee, 2007.

5   Chapman, Paul and Templar, Simon. *Measuring Retail Shrinkage: Towards a Shrinkage KPI.* Brussels: ERP Europe, 2004, p. 4.

6   Purpura, Phillip P. *Retail Security Shrinkage and Protection.* Boston: Butterworth Heinemann, 1993, p. 103.

7   Hollinger, Richard and Adams, Amanda. *2007 National Retail Security Survey Final Report.* Gainesville: University of Florida, 2007.

8   Hollinger and Adams.

9   Geason, Susan and Wilson, Paul R. *Preventing Retail Crime.* Canberra: Australian Institute of Criminology, 1992.

10   Muller, Max. *Essentials of Inventory Management.* New York: American Management Association, 2003, p. 40.

11   For the purposes of this book, the abbreviations BCE (before the Common Era) and CE (after the Common Era) will be used.

12   The Oldest Writings, and Inventory Tags of Egypt. Matteessich, Richard. *Accounting Historians Journal*, I, vol. 29, 2002, pp. 195–209.

13   Matteesich, p. 198.

14   Luke 2: 1–4.

15   Original inventories of early New York Jews (1682–1763). Hershkowitz, Leo. *American Jewish History*, 4, vol. 90, 2002, pp. 385–449.

16   Have, O. Ten. *The History of Accountancy.* Palo Alto, California: Bay Books, 1976, p. 40.

17   American Institute of Certified Public Accountants (AICPA). Online 2006, www.aicpa.org/About+the+AICPA (cited 5 May 2009).

18   Redin, James. *A Brief History of Mechanical Calculators.* <www.xnumber. com/xnumber/mechanical2.htm#top>, November 2007.

19   Fishman, Charles. *The Wal-Mart Effect: How the World's Most Powerful Company Really Works—and How it's Transforming the American Economy.* New York: Penguin, 2006.

20   *What is ERP?* Klaus, Helmut and Rosemann, Michael and Gable, Guy. *Information Systems Frontiers*, vol. 2, 2000, pp. 141–62.

21   Brooks and Wilson.

22   Toasting to success. Doherty, Katherine. 2008, *Food Logistics*, pp. 24–7.

23   Bell, Jacob. *A Historical Sketch of the Progress of Pharmacy in Great Britain.* London: Beaufort House, republished READ Books, 2007.

24   Bell, Jacob.
      Watson, Nigel. *The Business of Adding Value: A Short History of the Christie Group.* London: Christie Group Plc, 2004.

25   *WIS International.* <www.wisintl.com> (cited 5 April 2009).

26   AJIS Japan website. *History.* <www.ajis-group.co.jp/corporate/history. html> (cited 5 April 2009).

27   Coben, Diana. *Adult Numeracy: Review of Research and Related Literature.* London: National Research and Development Centre for Adult Literacy and Numeracy, 2003, p. 9.

28   Kutz, p. 8.

PART II: FINANCE

5: Financial reporting

All active enterprises around the world operate within legal environments, requiring generally accepted rules for accounting and reporting of commercial and financial activity. While accounting rules may vary from one regime to another, a set of common financial statements in various formats is always used to report on the health and performance of an enterprise.

This section considers the role of the inventory in regard to financial reporting, shrinkage measurement and stock valuations. The impact of inventory valuation error is examined, also its effect on the accuracy of financial reporting. Lastly, other forms of inventories and stock counts are considered in respect to financial reporting. This includes cyclic counts, auditor sampling and fixed asset registers.

5.1   Financial statements

Modern accounting is based on the 15th century notion that the sum of all debits should equal the sum of all credits.

This simple idea can be expanded into the foundational accounting equation:

$$A + E = L + E_o + R$$

Where:
A = asset
E = expense
L = liability
E_o = owner's equity
R = revenue

In double-entry bookkeeping, assets and expenses are debit accounts and represent financial resources used by the enterprise. Liabilities, owner equity and revenues are credit accounts representing an enterprise's sources of funds. From this equation the major financial statements are derived:

- the balance sheet
- the income statement
- the statement of cash flow
- the statement of retained earnings.

These statements provide an overview of the health of an enterprise in both the short and long term. Among enterprise assets, stock is often considerable. Within the financial statements it is essential that stock is reported accurately since it has implications for the viability and value of the enterprise.

Balance sheet

The balance sheet represents a snapshot of all assets, liabilities, equity and accumulated profit for an enterprise on a given date. The simple accounting equation can be rearranged to represent the balance sheet, where expense is moved to the other side. Profit or loss (PL) is defined as the difference between revenue and expense within a defined period.

$$A = L + E_o + R - E = L + E_o + PL$$

Since stock is a traded asset it represents real money, requiring capital to purchase and generating liquidity when sold. Purchased stock generates liabilities from creditors and consumes cash assets as creditors are paid. Accordingly the value of held stock is included as a current asset on the balance sheet.

Income statement

The income statement represents a subset of the general accounting formula. The accumulated profit or loss within a period is equal to revenue less expenses (or PL = R – E). The profit part of PL is often called 'net profit' since it is the remaining amount after considering all revenues and less all expenses such as stock purchases, all business overheads and interest. It is also often referred to as the 'bottom line'.

A subset of net profit used by merchandisers and manufacturers that hold and sell stock is gross profit (GP). Gross profit represents only the difference between stock sales revenue and the cost of the goods. It reflects the gross margin made on the sale of stock and excludes other enterprise expenses like wages, rent or other operational costs. It is defined as:

$$GP = \text{sales revenue} - \text{cost of goods sold}$$

Gross profit is often expressed as a percentage of total sales (where: GP / Sales × 100 = GP%)

The cost of goods sold (COGS) is calculated in one of two ways:

- The periodic inventory method calculates the COGS by taking the opening stock value at the period start, adding all purchases at cost during the period and deducting the closing stock value at the end of the period (where COGS = opening stock + purchases – closing stock). Stock counts are usually completed to determine the opening and closing stock valuations.
- The perpetual inventory method requires an accurate perpetual stock system where the perpetual inventory and COGS are automatically updated as stock is sold.[1]

The periodic inventory method uses stock counts to physically verify and value the stock. This approach has its advantages as it is independent of the enterprise trading records. However, stock counts are costly, time-consuming and must be completed at accounting period-ends.

The convenient advantage of the perpetual inventory method is that the COGS is calculated 'perpetually' as stock is traded. It is available anytime. The limitation of the perpetual stock system is that it assumes the perpetual inventory always represents the physical stock. Apart from recorded sales and purchases, other changes to the stock due to overages or shrinkage may not be accounted for adequately (see section 5.2 later in this chapter). Over time this can lead to potentially large variances between the true physical stock and the perpetual stock system's inventory.

With increasing computer technology most enterprises prefer the convenience of the perpetual inventory method. However, only by conducting periodic stock counts can the COGS be reported with reference to the physical stock, rather than theoretically using a perpetual inventory. For this reason, accounting standards and auditors generally require at least one stock count per annum to verify the perpetual inventory records and calculate the COGS (see Chapter 7).

Phar Mor inventory fraud

Blind faith in perpetual stock systems and inadequate stock counts can lead to 'surprises'—sometimes with disastrous results. A good example with catastrophic consequences was the 1992 Phar Mor case.

In the 1980s CEO Mickey Monus (with help from his CFO) built an empire consisting of some 300 Phar Mor drugstores across the US. Unfortunately, much of his apparent business success was due to his allegedly fraudulent overstatement of profits and inventory value. For around 10 years Monus misled his auditors and investors using two sets of books: one showing stellar performance and the other hiding huge losses.

Apparently Monus and his executives re-allocated losses to individual stores. They made false accounting entries including fake stock purchases, increasing inventory holdings, decreasing the cost of sales and over-counting stock.

Phar Mor's inventory shortages were concealed because their independent auditors examined the stock and inventories in only a few of the 300 stores and always announced which stores they would visit in advance. Then Phar Mor executives took the opportunity to always fully stock the few selected stores, while leaving the remaining stores below reported stock levels.

Eventually Phar Mor ran out of cash and the litany of financial anomalies was discovered with millions of dollars in losses. Monus was sentenced to prison and Phar Mor's auditors paid compensation in civil judgments for failing to identify the fraud.[2]

Cash flow and retained earnings statements

The cash flow (CF) statement refers to the amount of incoming and outgoing cash received and paid by an enterprise over a defined period such as a month or a quarter. It represents the likelihood that an enterprise can meet its debts and commitments in a timely manner and remain solvent at all times. Included in the CF statement is the opening cash and receivables plus the projected sales and other income, less any expenses over the defined period.

The other major remaining financial statement is the statement of retained earnings. This statement examines the changes in profit or losses, dividends paid, and other changes in retained profits.

While the stock value is not directly included in the cash flow or retained earnings statements, the trading of stock impacts them significantly. Since stock is an important current asset on the balance sheet, its accumulation consumes cash. This reduces an enterprise's liquidity and can affect profitability. Conversely, its reduction, although improving liquidity, can lead to 'out-of stock' items and as such can undermine customer satisfaction.

Sometimes stock suppliers offer big discounts to encourage bulk purchases. However, such price savings are often offset by additional handling and storage costs and increases the risk of stock expiry, obsolescence, theft, loss or damage during storage of the item.

The cost of capital is another factor when trying to balance stock levels. For an enterprise, the accumulation of stock decreases its available cash. This reduces its ability to meet other expenses like overheads or acquire other essential assets like equipment. Consequently, funding these activities requires loans or other forms of borrowings which can involve costly interest, further reducing profitability and solvency. Even if an enterprise has sufficient cash, spending it on unessential stock limits its use in other commercial opportunities.

In an effort to balance their cash flow some enterprises try to enforce short payment terms on their customers, while imposing longer payment terms on their suppliers. The difference serves as a cash 'float' and buffers the enterprise from the vagaries of often unpredictable supply and demand.

5.2 Shrinkage

Shrinkage refers to the difference between the actual stock value, based on a stock count valuation, and the theoretical stock value, given purchases and sales. Shrinkage is common to all stock holding enterprises, but most prevalent in retail environments where attractive and desirable stock is displayed for the public and employees to see and touch.

Shrinkage is not directly included in the financial statements, but since it reflects lost sales and represents a reduction in stock asset value, it affects both the PL statement and the balance sheet.

Aggregate shrinkage calculation

Retailers commonly measure shrinkage by taking the difference between the potential value of stock according to the sales and purchase records and the true value of stock according to a stock count. It is normally expressed as a percentage of their retail sales.

The theoretical retail stock value is determined by taking all retail sales over a given period, deducting all purchases valued at retail, and deducting the retail stock value at the start of the period. It reflects the stock valuation the enterprise should have in theory, given its starting stock value and trading for the period. It is expressed below using a simple formula:

$$\text{theoretical stock at retail} = \text{opening stock at retail} + \text{purchases at retail} - \text{sales at retail}$$

The actual retail stock value is derived by completing a stock count at the end of a period and determining a retail stock valuation:

$$\text{actual stock at retail} = \text{stock count valued at retail}$$

Shrinkage is the difference between the two and can be expressed as:

$$\text{shrinkage} = \text{theoretical stock at retail} - \text{actual stock at retail}$$

It is normally expressed as a percentage relative to sales at retail. Consider a simple example: an enterprise begins the year with a stock holding of $180,000 valued at retail. During the course of the year it purchases $1,040,000 of stock, and sells $1,000,000 of stock, all valued at retail. After a year of trade the remaining theoretical stock value will be:

$$\$1,040,000 + \$180,000 - \$1,000,000 = \$220,000$$

At the end of the trading year a stock count is also completed and the actual remaining stock valuation is $200,000 at retail.

Shrinkage is calculated as the difference between the actual stock and the theoretical stock, both valued at retail. In this case shrinkage is:

$$\$220,000 - \$200,000 = \$20,000$$

This $20,000 shrinkage can also be expressed as a percentage relative to the total retail sales over the same period:

$$\$20,000 \, / \, \$1,000,000 \times 100 = 2\%.$$

Note that shrinkage can also be calculated relative to cost, where instead of valuing all variables at retail value, they are valued at cost. Retail shrinkage reflects the lost sales to the enterprise including profit, whereas cost shrinkage reflects only the lost stock valued at its cost.

Since stock holds financial value, shrinkage reflects lost money. All trading enterprises that hold stock typically suffer some shrinkage, so reducing the risk of stock shrinkage by improving the security of stock is critical. The opposite of shrinkage is called 'overage', and it occurs when the actual stock value is higher than the theoretical stock value.

Overages are rare but can sometimes occur, for instance, in large manufacturing and logistics environments. Stock stored in the wrong location and written-off previously may be found during a stock count and returned to the stock-on-hand (SOH). Although the net effect is not actually an increase in stock across periods, it does represent an increase in stock if the second period is considered on its own. Note also that bonus stock is technically not an overage, but ordinary stock received at no cost. Unfortunately shrinkage is more common and occurs when stock has been stolen, damaged or recorded in error.

Item shrinkage calculation

Calculating the total shrinkage for all stock is helpful but it does not identify which specific items were lost. By contrast, perpetual stock systems that monitor stock at an item level are able to identify shrinkage by item. The following example highlights this approach.

Figure 5.1 provides a simple inventory of only six items and a total of 100 units. The inventory includes the item number, description and quantity and also includes two additional fields for lost and damaged stock.

Theoretical			Actual		
Item	Retail	SOH qty	Lost $	Damaged	SOH qty
1	$ 2.50	10	3	–	7
2	$ 1.15	20	–	1	19
3	$ 3.00	30	1	–	29
4	$ 4.20	12	1	–	11
5	$ 3.70	22	–	3	19
6	$ 2.00	6	–	–	6
Totals		100	5	4	91

Figure 5.1: Inventory table showing theoretical, lost, damaged and actual stock quantities for six items.

The theoretical SOH quantity is based on the perpetual inventory records derived from sales and purchase history. The total actual SOH quantity is derived from item stock counts used to verify and update the quantity on hand, lost and damaged stock.

Stock with item numbers 1, 3 and 4 have been lost. For item number 1, the quantity lost is high relative to its stock level (3 were lost from a quantity of 10 or 30%). This might be because the item is highly desirable, or perhaps poorly secured, and thus prone to theft. Similarly, item number 5 has a quantity of 3 damaged, suggesting that it is prone to breakage, possibly because it is stored unsafely.

Figure 5.2 shows the shrinkage at an item level for the same 6 items. The total quantity and value at retail for the lost items is 5 units with a value of $14.70. The total potential stock value is $281.80. The shrinkage, in dollars, is the difference between the potential and actual stock values which is $26.95 ($14.70 + $12.25).

The benefit of the perpetual stock system is that the shrinkage can be tracked during a period and reviewed over time. Separate reports can be generated indicating problem areas, such as items with the highest rate and the type of stock loss. Such identifiable item level stock shrinkage issues can then be easily and promptly addressed.

	Theoretical		Actual						Shrinkage
Retail	SOH qty	Qty $	Lost	Lost $	Dmgd	Dmgd $	SOH qty	Qty $	
$2.50	10	$25.00	3	$7.50	–	$0.00	7	$17.50	$7.50
$1.15	20	$23.00	–	$0.00	1	$1.15	19	$21.85	$1.15
$3.00	30	$90.00	1	$3.00	–	$0.00	29	$87.00	$3.00
$4.20	12	$50.40	1	$4.20	–	$0.00	11	$46.20	$4.20
$3.70	22	$81.40	–	$0.00	3	$11.10	19	$70.30	$11.10
$2.00	6	$12.00	–	$0.00	–	$0.00	6	$12.00	$0.00
Totals	100	$281.80	5	$14.70	4	$12.25	91	$254.85	$26.95

Figure 5.2: Inventory table showing theoretical, lost, damaged and actual stock quantities and stock valuation for six fictitious items.

5.3   Valuation methods

Professional appraisers use one of three broad methods to value any asset. These are the cost approach, income approach and market approach.

The cost approach

The cost approach values an asset by determining the current price for the same or similar asset. The price of the similar asset may be adjusted to allow for any differences in features or utility, physical deterioration or functional and economic obsolescence. This approach is often used in the insurance industry. For example, a two-year old washing machine is destroyed in a fire. Its value might be determined by establishing the new price for the same or similar model, and adjusting the price given its age.

The income approach

The income approach values an asset using the present value of its future economic benefits. It determines the likely income or yield that the asset will provide (including earnings, cost savings, tax deductions, and disposal value) and from which it determines a likely current or present value. Manufacturing machinery is sometimes valued in this manner. A piece of equipment is worth its likely income, less service costs over its expected functioning life.

The market approach

The market approach values an asset based on market evidence between legitimate, independent purchasers and sellers in a genuine and free market. Most residential real estate is valued in this way, where a property's value may be derived by comparing it to other similar and recent property sales.

Stock in a solvent and trading enterprise will be valued using the cost approach. That is, the source of the stock valuation is the price paid to its various suppliers to acquire it. This is the value that is recorded in the perpetual stock system. Rarely, in special circumstances, might a different valuation method be used. This depends on the circumstances or purpose of the valuation.

5.4   Valuation purpose

Business and asset valuations will vary in time and under different circumstances. Macro-economic factors, supply and demand and enterprise performance will all affect the perceived value of an enterprise and its assets. This is also true of physical stock within an enterprise. Its value will change depending on the timing and circumstances of the valuation.

Perpetual stock systems provide a reliable means to store one or more stock prices. These can be used to value stock in different circumstances and for different purposes. Below are listed some of the common valuation concepts.

Finance valuations

Financial reporting requires the valuation of all assets held by an enterprise including its physical stock. The stock valuation appears in the balance sheet (BS) and is needed to calculate the cost of goods sold and gross profit used in the income statement (IS).

Financial stock valuations generally use an item's cost (purchase) price to determine its stock value. However price inflation, seasonal fluctuations, bulk discounts, rebates, and tax changes can all affect the price of an item over a relatively short period. In practice, separate purchases of the same item may have been bought at different prices.

Keeping track of the exact price is difficult, even with a perpetual stock system. To simplify matters, there are four common methods to maintain prices used to value stock for the purpose of financial reporting:

- **last in, first out (LIFO)** assumes all stock quantities are valued with their most recent price
- **first in, first out (FIFO)** assumes all stock quantities are valued with their first or earliest recorded price

- **weighted average** uses an average price based on the number of units bought with that price
- **exact pricing** uses the exact acquisition price for each item.

Of the pricing methods above, the one that generates the most interest and controversy is LIFO. As a valuation method, LIFO adjusts all stock for price inflation. Using historical prices can often undervalue stock (i.e. value at less than its replacement cost), which inflates gross profit and can mislead stakeholders on true profitability. Alternatively, cost calculations using the most recent price can cause the cost of goods sold to be higher, lowering gross profit. Thus, the LIFO method has the advantage of lowering an enterprise's tax liability, and it is a commonly accepted method in some countries where it is a legal tax avoidance strategy. In other countries the use of LIFO is prohibited in gross profit calculations and another pricing method such as the average price or exact pricing must be used.[3]

Market value

While the term 'market value' is used widely, particularly for the valuation of realty and plant and equipment, its exact meaning will vary from one appraiser to another. It depends on their professional association and source definitions.[4] For example, there are subtle differences between a host of similar terms such as: market value, fair value, going concern value and market value for existing use.[5]

The market value of stock, sometimes called stock at valuation (SAV), is used when a going concern enterprise is sold from one party to another. In these circumstances, stock is valued at the price needed to replace the stock at the date of the sale. Accordingly, the LIFO value is often used since it reflects a most recent and available cost price.

Although a market and financial valuation may use the same prices and therefore derive the same stock value, they are each based on different assumptions. A market valuation of physical stock assumes that the prices used:

- reflect the SOH at the date of valuation when the transaction took place

- reflect an open market and arms-length transaction without either party suffering undue duress or time pressure
- include all taxes, delivery costs and associated put-away costs
- reflect the buying power of the enterprise and are appropriate for the stock quantities acquired (where all discounts and rebates are applied appropriately)
- reflect the condition of the stock (where used, obsolete and damaged stock is disregarded or discounted).

A perpetual stock system is sometimes used to generate the market valuation of stock. However with a sale of business, in order to provide transparency and ensure that the perpetual system is correct, the parties usually insist on an independent stock count close to or on the date of sale. During the stock count damaged, obsolete or lost items can be excluded, ensuring the subsequent stock valuation is more accurate and current. Typically the price of the items used in the stock valuation are drawn from the perpetual stock inventory and agreed on by both parties, whereas the actual stock items and quantities are taken from the independent stock count inventory.

Reinstatement value
The reinstatement value of stock is used for insurance and stock security purposes. This valuation describes the cost to replace the stock holdings with identical or similar stock, with the same condition and utility, and in the same physical location. It includes the cost price and all tax, transport and delivery costs.

The reinstatement valuation is often used to determine the level of insurance cover required in the unlikely event that the stock is destroyed by fire or lost by theft. In practice, insurers and banks will use the stock valuation from the financial balance sheet to approximate this, even though they are potentially different. The financial valuation may, for example, only include the stock cost and not associated transport and put-away costs.

Salvage value

Salvage or forced sale value is the amount which may reasonably be received from the sale of stock when it is sold in haste by an unwilling seller. The salvage value is typically used when an enterprise is no longer solvent and enters into receivership or bankruptcy. In this case, all assets—including stock—may be 'liquidated' in a short space of time, and the normal stock sale process for the enterprise will not be used.

Once an enterprise is no longer a going concern, the realizable stock value is often only a fraction of its original cost. In these circumstances using a price drawn from a perpetual inventory may not be representative of the stock's value. Stock sold at salvage value is commonly reported in the media and is a frequent reason to market.[6] In such circumstances it is common for the salvage value to be only a small proportion of the stock's original price.

5.5   Summary

Stock value and financial statements

Stock is an asset and its value is included in an enterprise's financial statements. The stock valuation is reported as a current asset in the balance sheet and is used in the income statement to determine the cost of goods sold (COGS):

$$(COGS = opening\ stock + purchases - closing\ stock)$$

from which gross profit (GP) is calculated:

$$(GP = sales\ revenue - COGS)$$

Periodic stock counts and perpetual inventory valuations

Stock can be valued periodically using a stock count or at any instance in time using a perpetual stock system to generate a perpetual inventory. The stock count valuation is considered an 'actual' value of stock since it is based on a physical count of the stock, whereas a perpetual inventory valuation is considered a 'theoretical' valuation because it is based on the stock that should be held, given sales, purchases and transfer records.

Shrinkage

Stock count valuations are used by merchandisers to determine stock shrinkage over an accounting period. Shrinkage is usually valued at retail and is the difference between the theoretical stock valuation (usually calculated using a perpetual inventory) and the actual stock holding (generated using a stock count).

Valuation purpose

Stock counts and perpetual inventories are often used to generate valuations for specific purposes including:

- market value at the transfer of business ownership
- reinstatement value for insurance and finance security
- salvage value at an insolvency or forced sale.

6: Stock valuation error

Stock valuations are used to prepare enterprise financial statements and report asset value, shrinkage and profits to stakeholders including managers, shareholders, purchasers, insurers and financiers. Perpetual and stock count inventories are frequently used to generate stock valuations. Stock valuations are calculated by summing the products of each item price and quantity. This means that the accuracy of the valuation relies on the accuracy of the inventory from which the item prices and quantities are drawn. In this chapter the impact of some common types of stock valuation error are considered.

6.1 Valuation cut-off error

While a stock count can be use to establish or verify an inventory, care must be taken to ensure that it includes only the appropriate stock at the correct instant in time. Accounting period-end timing disparities between the physical stock and the computer system that maintain the stock inventory are common.

Perpetual inventories represent the theoretical physical stock at an instant in time. Ideally, stock movements (purchases, sales and transfers) are entered into the computer system as they occur and the perpetual inventory is instantly updated. However, in practice disparities occur when the physical stock quantity is altered before or after its corresponding transaction is recorded in the inventory. This is particularly problematic at period cut-offs where stock transactions may be processed in one period and the physical stock processed in another.

Similar problems are common during stock counts. Recent stock deliveries may be counted that have not yet been received into inventory. Alternatively, items may be incorrectly counted that were already sold, processed and waiting for dispatch.

Examples of on-site stock cut-off issues include:
- stock sold and invoiced but still on-site
- stock received on-site but not yet recorded
- stock held on-site for others
- consignments to be purchased as used or sold.

Off-site stock examples that should be included in an inventory include:
- stock held at other sites and locations
- stock in transit
- stock with customers or vendors, but not billed
- consignments held by others until used or sold.

There are also other item categories to be considered which should be recorded in the inventory but may not be included in a stock valuation, for example:
- **Holds**: items separated from normal trading stock but not yet purchased by a client are technically stock and should be included in the valuation and inventory.
- **Consignment**: items owned by a third party that may be included in the inventory, but should be excluded from a stock valuation.
- **Obsolete**: expired, damaged or obsolete items are sometimes included in the inventory but should be excluded in a stock valuation. Ultimately they should be written-off, adding to shrinkage unless a supplier will replace them at no cost.
- **Returns**: items that are returned and refunded should be included in a stock count, but if they are damaged or unsaleable, they should be excluded and written-off.

6.2   Valuation pricing error

Even if the inventory item quantity is accurate, if the pricing is wrong, the valuation will be wrong. Some common sources of pricing error are:

- **Keypunching**: where the data are unintentionally entered incorrectly.
- **Calculation**: where the conversion of carton size to unit size is incorrect or the wrong carton units are used.
- **Local taxes**: where the wrong taxes are applied. Consumption taxes such as goods and services tax (GST) or value-added tax (VAT) should be excluded from an inventory price as they only apply when the item is sold. By contrast, wholesale taxes and freight costs are included, as these fees and charges contribute to the landed cost of the item.
- **Free stock:** where free samples, bonus stock and purchase rebates are ignored, inflating the average item value.

6.3   Valuation error and COGS

Despite best efforts, any inventory and corresponding stock valuation will arguably contain some error. The impact that this stock valuation error will have on the financials will vary depending on its magnitude relative to other variables.

Stock valuation error and stock turns

A useful statistic for an enterprise is to count the number of stock turns per year. Stock turns refers to number of times that the average stock holding has been sold over a fixed period such as a year. It can be calculated using the formula:

$$\text{number of stock turns} = \text{COGS} / \text{average inventory}$$

To illustrate, consider an enterprise with an opening stock of $90,000, and a closing stock of $110,000. This corresponds to an average stock value of $100,000 (since ($90,000 + $110,000) / 2 = $100,000).

Given purchases of $600,000, the number of stock turns in the period is 5.8 (since ($90,000 + $600,000 – $110,000) / $100,000 = 5.8 turns).

Comparable enterprises with a higher number of stock turns are more efficient, since they effectively minimize their stock holdings by replacing them in close synchronization to actual sales. Now, consider the stock valuation and the COGS. Recall that gross profit (GP) is calculated by deducting sales from the COGS. And the COGS is equal to the purchases adjusted by the opening and closing stock:

$$(GP = \text{Sales Revenue} - \text{COGS}; \text{where}$$
$$\text{COGS} = \text{Opening Stock} + \text{Purchases} - \text{Closing Stock}).$$

Any error in the opening and closing stock values will have little impact on the GP if they are small relative to purchases, because any stock valuation error will be absorbed by the much larger volume of purchases when there are a high number of stock turns per year.

Consider an enterprise with annual sales of $900,000, purchases of $600,000, an opening stock of $100,000 and closing stock of $100,000. The resulting COGS would be $600,000 ($100,000 + 600,000 – $100,000) and the GP would be $300,000 ($900,000 – $600,000).

The purchases are six times the closing stock value ($600,000/ $100,000). In other words, there are six stock turns in a year. Figure 6.1 highlights the GP as a percentage of sales. Now, even if the stock value is $10,000 too high (10%), it will only inflate the GP by 3.44% (($300,000 / $290,000 – 1) × 100 = 3.44%) because the error in the stock value is still much smaller than the relatively larger stock purchases and sales.

On the other hand, if the same enterprise had the same stock valuation error, but with relatively smaller purchases and sales, its impact on the calculation of gross profit would be far greater.

COGS	=	OS	+	Purchases	–	CS
$610,000		$100,000		$600,000		$90,000
$600,000		$100,000		$600,000		$100,000
GP	=	Sales	–	COGS		
$290,000		$900,000		$610,000		
$300,000		$900,000		$600,000		

Figure 6.1: Effect of stock valuation error on gross profit when sales and purchases are relatively high compared to stock value.

Figure 6.2 highlights the GP as a percentage of sales where stock purchases are $60,000 and sales are $90,000.

COGS	=	OS	+	Purchases	–	CS
$70,000		$100,000		$60,000		$90,000
$60,000		$100,000		$60,000		$100,000
GP	=	Sales	–	COGS		
$20,000		$90,000		$70,000		
$30,000		$90,000		$60,000		

Figure 6.2: Effect of stock valuation error on gross profit when sales and purchases are relatively low compared to stock value.

In this case, the number of stock turns is only 0.6 ((100,000 + $60,000 − $100,000) / $100,000) = 0.6). Now if the stock value remains $10,000 too low (10%) it will inflate GP by 50% (($30,000 / $20,000 − 1) ×100 = 50%). This is because the magnitude of the stock valuation error is relatively large compared to the stock purchases and sales.

Stock valuation error and profit margin

Now, consider stock valuation error in regard to stock profit. An item's sale price less its purchase price is its profit. This can be expressed as a percentage relative to its sales price (mark-down) or relative to its purchase price (mark-up). Another term used to describe profit relative to its sales price is profit margin. It can be calculated using the formula:

$$\text{(sales price − cost price) / sales price} \times 100 = \text{profit margin \%}$$

The larger the profit margin, the less stock valuation error will affect GP. Figure 6.3 illustrates two scenarios for one type of stock item. In the first, the closing stock quantity should be 100 but is overstated by 20 units, making it 120 units. In the second, the opening (OS) and closing stock (CS) quantities are the same (100). The item cost price is $100 and the retail price is $200, giving a 50% profit margin on each unit sold (($200 − $100) / $200 × 100 = 50%)).

COGS	=	(OS	+	Purchases	−	CS)	×	Cost
$53,000		(150		500		120)		$100
$55,000		(150		500		100)		$100
GP	=	(Units	×	Retail)	−	COGS		
$47,000		500		$200		$53,000		
$45,000		500		$200		$55,000		

Figure 6.3: Example of stock quantity error and its impact on gross profit when the item profit margin is large.

In this example there is a 4.4% (($47,000 / $45,000 – 1) × 100) error in GP if the high profit margin item has a 20% stock count error.

However, if the same quantity error is observed for an item with a lower profit margin, it has a much larger impact on GP. Figure 6.4 illustrates two scenarios for one type of stock item. In the first scenario, there is a quantity error in the closing stock of 20 units. In the second scenario, the OS and CS quantities are the same. The item cost price is $100 and the retail price is $120, giving a 20% profit margin on each unit sold (($125 – $100) / $125 × 100 = 20%).

COGS	=	(OS	+	Purchases	–	CS)	×	Cost
$53,000		(150		500		120)		$100
$55,000		(150		500		100)		$100
GP	=	(Units	×	Retail)	–	COGS		
$9,500		500		$125		$53,000		
$7,500		500		$125		$55,000		

Figure 6.4: Example of stock quantity error and its impact on gross profit when the item profit margin is small.

In this example there is a 27% (($9,500 / $7,500 – 1) × 100) error in the GP if the low profit margin item has a 20% stock count error.

Figures 6.3 and 6.4 illustrate that any stock quantity error will affect the stock valuation, COGS and, ultimately, the GP. Its impact will depend not only on the magnitude of the error, but also on the magnitude of its profit margin. When profit margins are small, stock valuation error will affect GP much more than when margins are large.

6.4   Summary

Stock valuations
Perpetual and stock count inventories are frequently used to generate stock valuations. Stock valuations are essential to prepare financial documents and report the commercial performance of an enterprise. Unfortunately stock valuations inevitably include some error due to the magnitude and complexity of trading and record-keeping.

Stock valuation error
An inaccurate inventory will distort an enterprise's financial results. Stock valuations may be incorrectly reported and too much or too little tax paid on profits. Common causes of stock valuation error are:

- the application of incorrect period cut-offs where physical stock is inadvertently included or excluded in valuation calculations
- the incorrect treatment of holds, consignment, returns and obsolete stock
- there is incorrect item quantity and pricing, often due to key-punching, calculation, tax, size and bonus errors.

While stock valuation accuracy depends on the correct inventory quantity and cost price across all items, its impact on the COGS depends on its relative magnitude compared to the sales and purchases. Stock valuation error is relative but it will have a lesser impact on the calculation of GP if the profit margin is large or the opening and closing stock values are small relative to the volume of stock purchases.

7: Partial stock counts

An inventory may not represent all stock, but may be a subset of the stock or a partial inventory. There are a number of circumstances in which a partial stock count is completed to establish or verify a partial inventory.

7.1 Cyclic versus full stock counts

Cyclic stock counts are a type of partial stock count where a portion of the stock is selected and counted. Typically the entire stock is separated into sections based on locations or categories and each section is counted at least once over a given cycle, say quarterly or annually. Ostensibly the cyclic inventory is equivalent to a full stock count since all sections are counted, but the stock count is spread over much more time—a cycle.

At a minimum all enterprises are required to complete at least one stock count per year to verify the perpetual inventory and to establish a transition valuation between financial periods. However, many enterprises choose to verify their perpetual inventory more than once per year. Despite the cost, due to their trading volumes, enterprise policy or risk of stock loss, they conduct more frequent stock counts.

Cyclic stock counting provides a strategy to identify and frequently verify stock that is prone to inventory inaccuracy. Consider an enterprise that completes two full stock counts each year. In practice this means the full inventory is checked once every six months. However, a large proportion of items are of low value with low velocity (i.e. few stock turns). This stock only requires an annual stock count. By contrast, a smaller proportion of remaining stock is of high value and/ or high velocity. This stock may be at higher risk of theft, damage or error and thus requires more frequent stock counts.

By conducting two full stock counts each year, the enterprise is over-checking the low value and low velocity items, while under-verifying the riskier and error-prone remaining stock.

Figures 7.1 and 7.2 provide examples where the frequency of cyclic stock counting is proportional to the stock error risk. Imagine dividing a stock holding into nine equally-sized item categories according to stock value and velocity. Using full stock counts, on average all items may be counted twice per year, with 18 section counts. But using cyclic stock counts, the high-risk items can be counted more frequently; this improves enterprise inventory accuracy and security with the same 18 section counts each year.

	High $	Medium $	Low $	Total section counts
Fast moving	2	2	2	6
Medium moving	2	2	2	6
Slow moving	2	2	2	6
Total item counts	6	6	6	18

Figure 7.1: Number of section counts when 2 full stock counts are completed.

	High $	Medium $	Low $	Total section counts
Fast moving	4	2	2	8
Medium moving	3	2	1	6
Slow moving	2	1	1	4
Total item counts	9	5	4	18

Figure 7.2: Number of section counts when selective cycle counts are used.

Strategic cyclic counting spends the same resources and focuses more counting effort on the areas of highest risk.

Many books and authors have argued the merits of regular cyclic counting in preference to more infrequent full stock counts.[7] Below is a summary of the main arguments in support of both methods.

The advantages of cyclic stock counts in preference to full stock counts include:

- **Strategic:** selective cyclic stock counts ensure stock of high value, risk or turnover can be counted more frequently than less problematic stock, maximizing stock count impact and minimizing effort.
- **Convenience**: large enterprises with vast stock holdings and little opportunity to stop all stock movements may find it difficult to schedule enough workers and time to complete a full count. Cyclic stock counts can be conveniently scheduled around trading activity, employee levels and selected stock movements.
- **Cost effective**: Since cyclic stock counts can be efficiently scheduled around the enterprise, cost savings are likely to be made since high-risk inventories are more accurate, fewer sales are lost and stock cut-offs, overtime and labor costs are reduced.

The main advantages of the full stock count compared to the cyclic stock count include:

- **Completeness:** during cyclic stock counts, stock in different locations or categories may be easily missed or inadvertently double counted over time. For instance, the same items in multiple locations are easily overlooked, and stock period close-offs may be compromised where stock is unintentionally moved during or between cyclic stock counts. By contrast, during a full stock count all stock is counted. There is less opportunity for stock in separate locations or categories to be missed or double counted.
- **Timeliness:** typically the full stock count is completed when trading ceases and all stock is counted at the same time. It requires little post-inventory reconciliation and manipulation and is less affected by stock cut-offs and adjustments if it is

completed on or near the required stock count date. Accordingly, the full stock count can be more easily understood, audited and the process reviewed in a relatively short period.

- **Independence:** The full stock count can be performed without major reliance on an enterprise's existing perpetual stock system. Also, it can more easily be counted by a third party, since it requires less knowledge of specific stock locations or categories, and only requires access to the stock once during the full stock count.
- **Auditor and court preferred:** a full stock count is objective and repeatable on demand. Largely because of its completeness, timeliness and independence, it is usually the preferred means to verify inventory accuracy.[8]

Of course, cyclic stock counts and full stock counts are not mutually exclusive or polar opposites. Their concepts and methods are fundamentally the same and many enterprises use a mixture of both. For instance, cycle stock counting can be used during the year and a full stock count completed at year's end.

7.2   Auditors and the stock count

Sample stock counts are another common form of partial stock count. Sample counts are often conducted during an annual financial audit as a means to check the veracity of a full stock count. They are effectively a diagnostic tool to gauge the likely accuracy of the stock count.

The process usually requires a professional auditor to attend an enterprise's full stock count. The auditor systematically selects stock items to count and compares their counts with those observed in the concurrent full stock count. Any discrepancies are recorded and reported.

Of course, to be statistically representative a sample stock count must proportionally reflect all of the stock items, not just a small select group. The statistical nature of representative sampling is described more fully in Chapter 19.

A small error in an inventory can create a large variance in its stock valuation. This in turn can cause major inaccuracies within important financial reports. For this reason accounting auditors are required as part of the financial audit of an enterprise to inquire and verify that the stock value, level and condition observed on-site is accurately reported in the inventory and the financial records.

Guidelines vary slightly between the major accounting firms, but they broadly recommend an auditor be present during a stock count and that they complete a number of systematic observations and checks. For instance, Ernst and Young's *Physical Inventory Observation Checklist* states:

> The purposes of the physical inventory observation are to determine that 1) the inventory [the stock] physically exists, 2) stated quantities fairly represent the actual quantities on hand at the date of the observation, and 3) the inventory [the stock] is in a usable and saleable condition (e.g., not damaged or obsolete). [9]

In practice, these requirements demand a significant amount of work from the auditor. It takes a high degree of professional experience to evaluate the likely risk and impact any inventory error will have on the enterprise. Just consider the task: any enterprise that has an independent audit is likely to have a substantial stock holding. The stock will be specialized, reflecting the industry that it serves. The inventory detail and accuracy depends on the enterprise systems and process it uses to manage and detail the inventory. The auditor must be able to decide if there is any error in the inventory, and whether this has any material impact on the veracity of the financial statements for which they certify.

When determining the stock value, accounting standards and inventory audit guidelines recommend a full stock count on or as near the period cut-off date as possible, rather than relying on a perpetual inventory or cyclic count records.

This makes sense, as a transparent stock count is relatively easy to witness and spot-check, compared to analyzing the veracity of a perpetual inventory valuation, which can be based on any number of individual transactions over an indefinite trading period.

Broadly, when considering the nature of the stock, the check methods available to the auditor consist of:

- viewing the physical stock (to see the type, layout and preparation)
- viewing the stock count process (to see that it is truly being counted)
- reviewing the stock count instructions (to ensure the process is transparent, sound, accurate and efficient)
- interviewing the stock count manager and any participants (to ensure they understand the task and are conscientious in their duties)
- checking the cut-off procedures (to ensure only the correct stock is included in the stock count)
- randomly sampling stock counts (to ensure the stock count actually reflects the inventory observed on-site).

These check methods are largely subjective and rely on the auditor to probe and ask questions that will identify shortcomings or risks in the process. Random sample counting is a statistical approach that is arguably more objective. Often, however, the samples chosen by the auditor are not actually random or large enough to be statistically representative.

Normally the auditor selects a sample of items on the shelf, recording each item number and quantity, and then compares this to the stock count inventory. This ensures that the stock on the shelf is correctly reported in the inventory.

The auditor then reverses the process and selects a sample of items from the inventory, recording each item number and stock count quantity, and then finds the corresponding item on the shelf. This ensures all items reported in the inventory actually exist on the shelf.

Any quantity discrepancy is deemed to be an error. That is, regardless of value or volume, there is a zero quantity tolerance for all items. (Chapter 19 reviews the statistics of sample sizes).

The stock count accuracy is acceptable if the error rate is less than 5% in the total number of sampled counts. So, if there were 30 sampled items and two or more counts disagree (2 / 30 × 100 = 6.6%), the stock count is considered inaccurate.

If the stock count is deemed inaccurate after the first sample, a further sample is taken and the test applied again. If the total error for both the first and second samples exceeds 10%, the stock count is again considered inaccurate and failed. So, to continue the example, a second random sample of 30 items is counted, and there is a discrepancy of 1 item. Given 2 errors in the first sample and 1 error in the second, there are 3 errors for 60 sampled items (30 in sample 1 and 30 in sample 2). Since 3 / 60 × 100 = 5% and, as this is less than 10%, the stock count is passed and accuracy is deemed to be greater than 90%.

In general, there are many benefits to this approach:
- It is fast and easy to perform; a relative novice can perform the test.
- It considers the relationship between the actual stock and the stock count inventory. By sampling in both directions it is testing that all stock is in the stock count, and that the stock count inventory represents the actual stock on the shelf.
- No assumptions are made about which items are to be checked as long as the items checked are thought to be representative.
- While the test is simple, it nonetheless instills a sense of the stock count being checked. This can motivate stock counters to take the task seriously and count the stock properly.
- It is most commonly applied to a stock count, but it can also be applied to the perpetual inventory as a 'quick and dirty' test of its accuracy.

There are also some serious weaknesses:
- Often the sample is surprisingly small, perhaps just a few items. This is not statistically representative of the inventory population the technique seeks to measure, and any conclusions can simply be wrong.

- The method assumes that the audit count is correct. In practice, the auditor may incorrectly count the stock and incorrectly report an error. Any reported error in the sample needs to double checked before it is considered a true error.
- The important data fields like stock location or product description are largely ignored in the test. If the item number and count match, the stock is considered correct.

7.3   Summary cyclic stock counts

Stock counts are essential to maintaining perpetual inventory accuracy, but they are disruptive and cost time and money. Cyclic stock counting is a partial stock count procedure that allows for stock with high value, high trading volumes or that which is prone to shrinkage, to be counted more frequently than slower moving more accurate stock. This improves overall perpetual inventory accuracy and saves time and cost.

Despite these advantages, full stock counts are preferred during audits, at sale of business, or at period-ends. This is because they are fully independent of the computer system and are more transparent to the observer.

Auditors and stock counts

Financial auditors are often required to witness stock counts in order to confirm: that the stock physically exists, that the inventory items, prices and quantities are accurate, and that the stock is usable, accessible and saleable.

Despite objective accounting techniques, the methods used to verify the stock count are largely subjective and rely on the auditor's experience and commonsense. Sample sizes are surprisingly small—often only a handful of items—and statistically these are unlikely to be representative of the stock. Nevertheless, the act of an auditor attending the stock count and checking some items probably motivates stock counters and improves the stock count. Managers and counters are likely to perform better if they know their work might be checked (see Chapter 4).

8: Asset registers

Much of this book has focused on the nature of the stock count and the perpetual inventory. Another inventory commonly maintained by various enterprises is the fixed asset register.

The term 'fixed assets' is largely used in accounting to refer to non-current assets held by an enterprise that cannot be quickly converted to cash. Fixed assets are in contrast to more readily realizable current assets like bank account cash, trade debtors and such. They are owned and held by an enterprise to facilitate production, merchandising or delivery of goods or services and unlike stock they are not held for sale in the course of trading.

International Accounting Standards (IAS 16) require enterprises to track and report their fixed assets in their financial statements. The standard defines fixed assets as those whose original cost can be measured and whose future economic benefit will flow into the entity. Examples include land and buildings, fixtures and fittings, plant, furniture, equipment, computers, software, patents, trademarks and such.

Generally, fixed assets have an operational life of more than a year. Over their serviceable life, in any given period, a portion of their value is deducted from their balance sheet value and charged (depreciated) to the profit and loss statement. Thus depreciation is an expense generated by the wear and tear or the diminution of an asset's historical value due to its usage. Eventually, at the end of its working life it will be valued at zero or some small salvage value.

Theoretically, not all fixed assets depreciate over time. Land, for example, often appreciates. However, for most fixed assets, its book value will decrease over time during its service life. Depending on its nature, accounting standards and rates of wear and tear, a number of models are used to reflect the fixed asset's decrease in value over time. Two common depreciation methods are:

- **Flat rate**: where a fixed proportion of the purchase price is deducted each year of the asset's effective life. For instance, a computer asset purchased for $1000 with an effective life of four years is depreciated 25% or $250 for each year over the term.

- **Reducing balance**: assumes that an asset loses more value during the earlier years of its life and accordingly is depreciated using a compound interest rate. For instance, the same computer with an effective life of four years is reduced in value by a compounding 30% each year and is respectively valued at $700, $490, $343, with a remainder of $240.

For many enterprises, their fixed assets comprise a large proportion of the value held on their balance sheet. Like stock, without these assets, the enterprise could not function and meet its operational obligations. Accordingly, it is in management's interest to ensure enterprise assets are monitored, secured, utilized and not damaged, lost or misappropriated.

Most financial computer systems have the facility to record assets as they are purchased and keep a detailed record of their historical and depreciated values. Financial computer systems largely focus on the accounting treatment of fixed asset purchases in a depreciation schedule. However, a depreciation schedule cannot be used for the management of assets as it rarely contains the required level of detail. Commonly, many enterprises use specific asset management software systems to establish and maintain their inventory of fixed assets.

Asset management systems consist of software user interface, a database and data transfer links to other financial computer systems. These systems uniquely number each asset and record basic details like the make, model, serial number, purchase date and price. They also store much more information, such as the asset category, supplier, hours-of-use, service history, warranty details, calibration requirements, cost center owner, allocated manager, linked or related assets, pooled assets and much more.

With such a rich database of fixed asset information, the systems can generate meaningful reports. For instance, the life and service cost of the same asset from two manufacturers can be compared and contrasted. Also, under-utilized or over-specified assets can be identified.

The inventory of fixed assets is often called an asset register. From time to time, often annually, the enterprise may choose to verify the physical existence of its fixed assets and reconcile these with the detail in the asset register. This process is akin to using the stock count to verify the physical stock and confirm the perpetual inventory record.

Asset definition

In order to establish an asset register the enterprise must first determine an asset definition. The asset definition describes what is to be considered an asset. Practical definitions vary depending on the nature of the asset, internal policies, prevailing economic conditions and local accounting standards.

Most definitions start with a minimum unique asset cost above which the asset will be capitalized and not expensed in a single financial year. This definition is then augmented for exceptions such as assets that are highly desirable and prone to theft or assets bought in quantity whose pooled value is greater than the minimum asset value threshold.

A good formal asset definition will be fairly clear but should also include examples for further clarity. For instance, assets to be capitalized and included on the asset register are as follows:

- Any single non-stock item with an operational life greater than 12 months and purchase price greater than $500. Inclusions are computers, furniture, software, hardware, carpets, plant, building improvements, carpets, wiring, patents, building fit-outs, licenses.

- Any single non-stock item with an operational life greater than 12 months and acquired in quantity with a total purchase price of $500. Inclusions are office chairs with a unit price of $250 and purchased in lots of two or more.
- Any item highly desirable and prone to theft. Examples include company mobile phones, external hard disk drives and small printers.

Note that this definition is included here for illustration. Specific definitions will vary depending on the enterprise's exact requirements. Any definition should include examples to ensure that those who use it can apply it consistently.

Data fields

Below are the names and some examples of common fields used and maintained in an asset register. Importantly, descriptions should be standardized so that key words can be searched and all examples found:

- Asset number: unique identifier, barcode label.
- Serial number: manufacturer's unique number.
- Description: standardized name, make, model, serial number.
- Date: purchase, manufacturer, warranty.
- Location: building, floor, room, etc.
- Cost centre: department, owner, etc.
- Condition rating (1: unserviceable, up to 5: brand new).
- Value: purchase price, reinstatement, depreciated, market, salvage.
- Service history: warranty details, service record.
- Photograph: asset in situ, invoice record.

Note that many fields will have different variants. For example, the asset register may support several value concepts including purchase, depreciated, market and salvage.

Asset register reconciliation

While a stock count is used to verify the perpetual inventory, a physical check of assets is conducted to ensure the veracity of the asset register. The asset check requires a review of all assets where asset numbers are recorded (or allocated if a number is not found) and additional details are recorded, like location, condition and perhaps a digital photograph.

Assigning barcodes or unique identifiers to assets improves the efficiency and accuracy of reconciliation. However, perhaps due to wear or recalcitrant behaviour, labels are sometimes lost, hidden, damaged or difficult to identify. This makes the task of reconciling observed assets in the field with those in the asset register difficult and tedious. Without a unique asset number to reconcile assets, each asset must be matched on other information.

After asset reconciliation, three reports can be generated.

- **Found and reconciled:** items found in the field and confidently reconciled with the existing asset register record.
- **Not found assets:** assets that exist on the asset register, but not confidently observed in the field.
- **New assets:** items found in the field, but not clearly identified on the asset register.

Clearly addressing the implications of not found and new assets is difficult for any enterprise. A loss of assets can represent a serious security issue or a problem with asset management and records. Within an asset management computer system new assets can be valued and added, whereas unfound assets can be marked as disposed due to theft or loss.

However, from a financial and accounting perspective the matter is more complex. Accounting standards have strict rules and policies regarding the write-off or addition of assets within the financial records. Generally, assets can only be added at their purchase value and only removed when sold for cash or fully depreciated and expensed against profits.

To avoid this dilemma, some enterprises maintain two asset registers. The first is the financial computer system which complies with the relevant accounting standards and maintains the depreciated asset values. The second is the asset management computer system which maintains other operational and historical asset details. Fortunately, as computer systems advance and asset policies grow more consistent, multiple inventories can be merged.

8.1   Summary

Fixed assets
The term 'fixed assets' refer to non-current assets held by an enterprise to facilitate production, merchandising or delivery of goods or services. The value of most fixed assets decreases over time during its service life. Most financial computer systems have the facility to record and maintain an inventory or asset register of fixed assets.

Asset registers
In order to establish an accurate asset a formal asset definition needs to be considered and adhered to. Common data fields included in the asset register are asset purchase and disposal details and purchase and depreciated value.

Asset reconciliation
Like a stock count, periodically enterprises should physically count and verify the accuracy of the asset register. An asset check will identify found, not found and new assets.

II: Notes

1   Juchau, R., Flanagan, J. and Mitchell, G. et al. *Accounting: Information for Decisions*. Melbourne: Thomson Learning, 2004.

2   Wells, Joseph T. Ghost Goods: How to spot phantom inventory. *Journal of Accountancy*, June 2001.

3   Juchau, Flanagan and Mitchell.

4   *International Valuation Standards 8th Edition.* London: International Valuation Standards Committee, 2007.

5   Dunckley, John. Financial Reporting Standards: Is market value for the existing use now obsolete? International valuation standards put into practice. *Journal of Property Investment & Finance*, vol. 18, no. 2, 2000, pp. 212–24.
    ISAB. *International Accounting Standard 16*. London: 2005.

6   King, Phillip and Rout, Miranda. Bargains galore after car dealer goes under. *The Australian*, 3 December 2008.

7   Brooks, R. B and Wilson, L.W. *Inventory Record Accuracy*. Hoboken New Jersey: John Wiley & Sons, 2007.
    Muller, Max. *Essentials of Inventory Management*. New York: American Management Association, 2003.
    Kutz, Gregory. *Executive Guide: Best Practice in Achieving Consistent, Accurate Physical Counts of Inventory and Related Property*. Washington: United States General Accounting Office, 2002, p. 6.
    Gumrukcu, Seda, Rossetti, Manuel D. and Buyurgan, Nebil. Quantifying the costs of cyclecounting in a two-echelon supply chain with multiple items. *International Journal of Production Economics*, 2008, vol. 116, pp. 263–72.

8   Ernst and Young. *Ernst and Young Physical Inventory Observation Checklist*, 2007.

9   Ernst and Young, p. 1.

PART III: TECHNOLOGY

9: Computer systems

The term 'logistics' refers to the systematic planning and implementation of resources necessary to sustain an enterprise; in particular the procurement, distribution and replacement of materials. The 'supply chain' is a related term referring to control of materials, information and finances as they move in a process from supplier to manufacturer, wholesaler, retailer and consumer.

The enterprises primarily concerned with logistics or supply chain management are those that are engaged in manufacture, distribution and retail. Today such enterprises rely on computer systems—both software and hardware—to facilitate their activities. In particular they use technology to maintain a perpetual inventory and monitor stock as it moves through the enterprise.

The rise of information technology solutions has transformed the logistics industry. In this technology section, manufacturing, distribution and retail inventory computer systems are examined. The underlying database and data fields are also considered. Finally, the role of data capture technology is reviewed, including handheld devices, barcodes and radio-frequency identification (RFID) tags.

9.1 Manufacturing inventory systems

Consider the tracking of stock in an enterprise around 100 years ago. Computers and the concept of the perpetual inventory did not yet exist. A ledger or inventory of critical and high-value items might be maintained at certain distribution points such as stock in reserve, production and finished goods. This inventory could be used to assist in production planning, but analysis of it was tedious and limited to the written record.

This changed with the development of computer inventory management systems that were capable of maintaining a perpetual inventory. By tracking each item over time at each location throughout the enterprise, stock levels could be better optimized and costs could be reduced.

Material requirements planning (MRP) refers to computer software systems, used primarily by manufacturers, to improve production planning, inventory control and manage the manufacturing processes. In particular, MRP systems consider seasonal and cyclic sales, supplier requirements and manufacture capacity, in order to save costs by reducing unnecessary stock levels and manufacturing duration.

In 1975 Dr Joseph Orlicky, a Czech-American engineer working with IBM, was an early advocate of MRP systems.[1] He recognized that efficient enterprises needed the right item and quantity at the right time.[2] Essentially, MRP systems are made up of two different elements: the master production schedule (MPS) and the bill of materials (BOM).

The MPS considers such questions as 'what, how many, and when?' It focuses on either long- or short-run outcomes. Short-run production schedules may describe the quantities of various items needed to fill current orders. Alternatively, long-term production schedules might describe the production capacity, employee requirements or money needed to meet and plan for demand over business cycles.

The MPS requires a number of inputs from enterprise databases including customer orders, seasonal and future demand expectations, inventory costs, production capacity, item and component lead-times and stock holding quantities.

The BOM is a list of the raw materials or components required to manufacture each item. It can describe multiple levels of components and their assembly. For instance, it will hierarchically list the parts needed to make a sub-component and describe how the sub-components combine to make a finished item.

Combining the MPS and the BOM information, the MRP system calculates and models the component quantities needed to produce a finished quantity in a given time. The MRP system primarily generates a schedule stating the time by which the production of each item and its components must be completed.

Since the development of MRP systems, the complexity of manufacturing planning systems has continued to evolve due to advances in computer hardware and manufacturing software. MRP theory and processes remain embedded in more modern manufacturing systems including manufacturing resource planning (MRP II) and just-in-time (JIT) stock management.[3] Increasingly, such manufacturing software systems are integrated with other organizational software modules to increase efficiency and functionality.

A weakness of MRP systems is their heavy reliance on masses of timely and accurate information, especially data relating to future demand.[4] In a business world filled with uncertainty, accurate demand information is not always available. However these systems do highlight the way in which an accurate inventory can be utilized to plan manufacturing schedules and minimize stock holding costs.

9.2 Distribution inventory systems

Stock distribution systems primarily track the flow of stock through one or more storage facilities. These systems seek to maximize the stock storage space and minimize the duration of stock receiving, storage, picking and dispatch. To do so the system provides and supports a perpetual inventory that describes and monitors each item and quantity in its location.

Stock location systems

Distribution inventory systems formally identify and label all stock storage locations. Fixed location systems allocate specific stock to the same fixed storage location, whereas random location systems allocate specific stock to any location as space and convenience permits.

Since stock in fixed location systems always live in the same location, employees soon learn where to find it. Stock can be stored in any convenient and practical location arrangement; whatever is most logical and functional for the enterprise.

Fixed location systems, however, consume space since the location must be large enough to accommodate the item's maximum volume, even if high stock levels are short term or infrequent. Consequently fixed location systems work best in largely static environments where stock varieties and quantities are stable over time.

Random location systems are useful in more dynamic environments where stock varieties and quantities are always changing. Stock is allocated to any location as needed. This is a very efficient way to maximize stock space. However, frequent stock location changes cannot be reliably learnt. Employees must always rely on the perpetual inventory to tell them where to locate and retrieve stock.

In practice, many enterprises use a hybrid location strategy with both fixed and random locations. Pallets are located randomly to maximize space and picking areas are fixed to facilitate frequent picks and replenishment.

Stock picking systems

Distribution inventory systems automate all aspects of warehouse stock control, particularly stock picking. In a simple system, an office operator receives an order (by telephone, email, etc.) and keypunches it into a computer. The system generates and prints a pick list in the warehouse. Warehouse operators systematically move from one location to another, selecting the required item and quantity, and ticking off the list as they work. The picked list is then keypunched into the computer updating the perpetual inventory.

More complex systems reduce the level of human involvement. Electronic stock picking systems operate in near real-time with little delay between picking and updating of the perpetual inventory. They are less prone to human error with little printing, operator searching or keypunching. These systems may include:

- Handheld devices using radio frequency to communicate with a central computer and direct an operator to the location of the proper stock for picking.
- Picking strips with lights at each location that the computer illuminates, telling the operator which location to pick from.

- Voice operator headsets where the operators verbally request the next item for picking, keeping their hands free to handle stock.

Some enterprises also implement systems which automate the stock picking process. While these have the potential to further reduce human error, they are costly to implement and are only commercially effective if the volume and manual picking costs are large enough to justify their installation. Examples include:

- Forklifts that are fixed in aisles and automatically pick and place stock in allocated pallet locations.
- 'A' frame stock dispensers (see Figure 9.1) where stock is stored in chutes on the outside of the A frame and automatically dropped into a box travelling along a conveyor underneath the frame.

Figure 9.1: Automated 'A' frame stock pick system.
(Courtesy Innovative Picking Technologies Inc.)

Distribution inventory systems vary greatly in complexity and automation. Importantly, each utilizes the perpetual inventory to distribute, locate and pick stock within the warehouse.

9.3   Point-of-sale systems

Point-of-sale (POS) systems facilitate and record customer transactions and support perpetual inventories. They are widely used in the retail and hospitality service industries.

A precursor to the modern POS was the cash register. Early devices from the late 19th century stored the money received from customers and summed consecutive sales which were then displayed numerically. Since the drawer would only open when a sale was made, they also served to reduce employee theft. Later a paper roll and print facility was added so receipts and a sales record could be provided. However these systems did not use or manage inventory information.

In the 1970s IBM introduced a centralized mainframe that communicated with store cash registers using peer-to-peer technology. It was effectively the first POS and pioneered the systematic collection, storage and analysis of itemized transactions. More modern POS systems communicate transaction data to 'back office' computers in small facilities or to 'enterprise information servers' for larger applications. The data is used to update and maintain a perpetual inventory at a local and group store level.

As technology improved, additional devices were integrated with the POS. These include barcode readers and electronic scales. Such devices reduced error-prone weighing and keypunching, improving sale speed and accuracy.

The POS system revolutionized retail business practices. For instance, in the hospitality industry it is not uncommon for the POS stations to be linked by a network to a central server computer for data storage. Small portable handheld computers with touch screens are used to collect orders from customers at tables. These orders are transferred to the server using radio frequency transmission and displayed on a large screen in the kitchen. The orders are also accessible from a computer hosted near the entrance where customer accounts are processed, billed, paid and receipts issued. Such systems have decreased order error and service time.

Supermarkets in recent years have introduced self-checkout POS facilities, allowing customers to self-scan or weigh their selected merchandise before paying using cash, credit or debit cards (see Figure 9.2). A single retail operator oversees several POS check-out facilities concurrently, and with a system of weight controls to alert the operator to discrepancies between the barcode of an item and its expected weight, the supermarket is able to control theft, improve customer traffic flow and reduce labor costs.

Modern POS systems maintain and facilitate an accurate perpetual inventory. As sales occur, information is collected relating to the products being sold, their quantities and prices. This information is used to adjust stock-on-hand values for each item as well as financial records, including the revenue generated by each item.

Figure 9.2: Example of a self-check-out POS system.

9.4 Merchandising systems

Historically, the manufacturer's and distributor's supply chain ended when their stock reached the retailer's receiving dock. Retailers used little science when considering the allocation of stock in their store, and the POS system only served to track items as they were sold and left the premises.[5]

But these days merchandising systems integrate a number of software technologies and data sources to:

- Draw and store floor plans using computer-aided design systems and link this information to other sales and performance-related variables.
- Create planograms highlighting model stock fixtures and measurements including shelf dimensions and the allocation of stock at an item and department level.
- Calculate the volume of merchandisable and non-merchandisable space and visually present stock sales, profits and other related data relative to the space used.

Floor plans

Merchandising systems allow inventory variables such as item number or department to be linked to store fixtures and then displayed on a floor plan. Such floor plan drawings can be used to create 'heat maps' by linking sales data to inventory space data. Figure 9.3 is an example of a floor plan integrated with sales data. Different color shades represent different levels of sales volume, with the darkest shades highlighting the fixtures generating the highest sales.

The heat map can clearly identify areas with low sales space productivity, a pattern that might not be discernible by trawling through sales data. By linking other variables to the fixtures such as shrinkage data, different heat maps can be created, for instance that may highlight areas prone to theft or inadequately monitored by security cameras. Floor plans can also be used to ensure products are placed in the aisle arrangements which best promotes sales.[6]

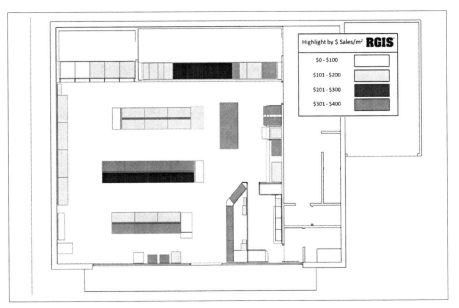

Highlight by $ Sales/m²	RGIS
$0 - $100	
$101 - $200	
$201 - $300	
$301 - $400	

Figure 9.3: Heat map of sales data for a small retail store. (Courtesy of RGIS Storplanner™.)

Planograms

Merchandising systems can also generate visual planograms of the stock. Planograms are elevation drawings or images of a fixture that indicate the sequencing and placement of stock on the shelf. Using an item's height, width and depth, it is possible to determine the shelf height required to fit each item, the number of facings that fit on a particular shelf, as well as the number of items in each facing.

Sales and marketing research can also be used to ensure particular products are placed at the most appealing height, with an efficient number of facings and with suitable item adjacencies.[7]

To be truly effective, merchandising systems require accurate information and consistent store level compliance. A well-designed planogram is useless if the space required for it is not available in the store or if store managers do not otherwise adhere to it.

Once a planogram is completed, an inventory of items can be printed in the order in which they appear on the shelf, which can then be used by retailers to ensure that fixtures are stocked correctly.

Space reporting

Merchandising systems ensure stock moves quickly and easily from the back of the store to the shelves and into customers' trolleys. Merchandising systems consider the nature of the stock, the physical store layout, customer demographics, and marketing in order to maximize stock attractiveness, functionality and sales. Whereas POS systems can report sales by item, merchandising systems can utilize sales information and report item sales relative to the space that items use.

For example, a retailer may discover the gross margin in one department exceeds another by 50%. However, when they calculate the merchandisable area used by each department (in square feet or meters) they realize that the poorer-performing department actually only requires half of the physical space. It is therefore a better performer than was first thought.

The gross margin return on space (GMROS) reflects the margins generated for the space consumed (where GMROS = gross margin \$ / area m²). Indeed, all item and department variables such as sales, shrinkage and gross margin can be considered relative to their space used.

Merchandising systems demonstrate how an accurate inventory can be used with space information to optimize stock appeal and sales.

9.5   Enterprise information systems

The term 'enterprise information system' (EIS) is generally reserved for large, integrated and modular computer software systems that operate across an entire enterprise.[8] Similar terms are enterprise systems (ES), enterprise applications (EA) and enterprise resource planning systems (ERP).[9]

Due to their size and complexity, enterprise information systems require considerable implementation and can cost millions of dollars.[10] Underlying the EIS is one or more shared databases. These consist of many tables, or files, which are linked by common key fields (such as the item number). The EIS is designed to securely handle and record potentially millions of transactions each day.[11]

It is possible to imagine the EIS as an intricate network of individual modules, each of which relate to a separate part of an enterprise's operations.[12] For a complex enterprise which controls all vertical elements of a supply chain, the modules may include manufacture, distribution and POS. Other modules may include human resources, accounts and finance.

Using a shared database, EIS brings a number of benefits:

- Information only needs to be entered once, reducing redundant, time-consuming and error-prone keypunching.
- Since all modules share the same data, reports are consistent and balance across modules.
- Access to up-to-date information across modules ensures that actions or decisions in different departments complement those made in other departments.
- Inventories can be maintained across modules, improving accuracy and reducing stock levels.
- Data mining and business intelligence tools can interrogate the database, gleaning new insights into the enterprise and its operations.

Consider an enterprise that manufactures, distributes and merchandizes stock. Using an EIS, the distribution center can track and forecast stock as it is manufactured. Likewise, daily retail sales can be sent and collected by a centralized data center and used to inform manufacturing about which stock should be produced or ordered from the warehouse.

In addition, the same data, purchases and sales will also be absorbed into financial systems and used to generate profit and loss summaries. Importantly, software report writers can produce additional reports, mining the database and selected data fields for hidden trends and insights without needing complex computer application programming. In this way, an enterprise can more easily assess the optimal quantity of particular items it requires at any location at any given time.

It is important to note that EISs are highly configurable and customized to suit the needs of different enterprises and industries; however, this flexibility makes it more difficult to analyze and compare systems in their entirety.[13]

9.6 Summary

A number of computer systems used in logistics and supply chain management were briefly reviewed in this chapter. Central to such systems is the establishment and maintenance of a perpetual inventory.

Manufacturing inventory systems such as MRP and MRP II manage the stock production schedule and ensure stock is produced in an efficient and timely fashion.

Distribution inventory systems manage the arrangement of stock within warehouse environments. They are responsible for ensuring stock is easy to store, access and retrieve, so that it may then be distributed to customers.

Point-of-sale systems (POS) facilitate and record customer transactions in retail settings. They ensure that transactions occur at the right price and are accurately recorded into the inventory.

Merchandising systems manage the placement of stock within retail environments. They ensure that shop floor space is used efficiently and that items are arranged in a way which maximizes sales.

Enterprise information systems (EIS) integrate a number of enterprise modules within a common database and share reporting and analysis.

10: Inventory databases

Today, the stock inventory is stored in an electronic database, allowing for fast and efficient item level storage and retrieval. A computer database consists of software known as a database management system (DBMS). The underlying database model or engine is commonly built upon relational rather than hierarchical concepts.

In relational databases, groups of information are arranged using common features or attributes. For example, a list of sales and purchase transactions might be arranged by the date they occurred. This means that each piece of information associated with a transaction such as the item number and price are represented in 'relation' to the transaction date.

Features that drive database technology and its utility include:

- **performance**, size in bytes of database and speed of storage and retrieval
- **concurrency**, safe transaction recording by concurrent users and applications
- **integrity**, all tables are linked using meaningful keys and conform to valid data types
- **security**, enforced access control, auditing, and encryption
- **recovery**, safe back-up and restoration after crashes, corruption or data-loss.

10.1 Database interface

The database interface refers to the manner in which data is received and sent from the computer system. Screen interfaces can be programmed and modified to suit each enterprise. Normally they are standardized and simplified to facilitate training and user-friendly data entry.

Increasingly, to avoid redundancy, data in an external system can be transferred to the EIS. A wide range of text and database formats can be easily specified and standardized to allow stable importing and exporting of data between computer systems and databases.

By accessing various inventory tables and fields, an inventory database can generate numerous reports which relate to different elements of an enterprise's operations. These reports are used extensively to identify inventory management issues, and are crucial to ensuring a business runs efficiently and effectively. Some common inventory table types and reports will be discussed in this chapter.

10.2 Database tables

Perpetual inventory systems are very complex and consist of hundreds of unique files or tables. Each table consists of fields (columns) and records (rows). Usually the first field holds a unique number (a key) that is used to identify each record and link multiple tables. The stock item number (or SKU) is an example of an essential key field used to identify stock items.

The particular information contained in each database table naturally varies. For example, transaction tables in a POS system record daily transactions at a store level. These include sales, purchases, transfers, write-offs, stock count adjustments and returns to supplier.

Apart from basic inventory data like the item number and quantity, transaction tables will store additional details including the sales operator, method of payment, amount paid, date and time, and so on.

Look-up and inventory tables are other common concepts used in most inventory management software systems. Look-up tables contain information that rarely changes and that is needed for reference from time to time. For example, the description, dimensions, weight and tax rate of a particular item may be contained in a look-up table.

Inventory tables contain current summary information about the stock. Figure 10.1 provides a simple example of a stock inventory table. Inventory tables are generated by processing transaction tables and accumulating and summarizing their details over selected periods. By storing transaction files indefinitely, inventory files can be re-generated in the event of a data-loss or as required for historical review. In so doing, the perpetual inventory is generated and maintained through time.

Date	Item #	Opening qty	Purchases	Sales	Write-off	Closing qty
1/01/2009	1	0	6	0	0	6
	2	0	6	0	0	6
	3	0	0	0	0	0
2/01/2009	1	6	0	2	0	4
	2	6	0	3	1	2
	3	0	2	0	0	2
3/01/2009	1	4	0	0	0	4
	2	2	12	6	0	8
	3	2	0	1	0	1

Figure 10.1: Stock inventory table summarizing simple stock transactions.

10.3 Reporting

Various reports can be generated in both printed and electronic formats by drawing on the information held in the perpetual inventory tables. This makes the populating and transfer of data between database systems easier and lends itself to more flexible data analysis. Common inventory reports include detailed sales, purchase and shrinkage histories by item, department and supplier. Such reports can provide powerful insights and identify simple inventory anomalies including:

- Negative stock holdings, where stock is being issued from the warehouse, but does not exist on the computer system.
- Stock pricing issues where stock has zero, negative or incorrect prices.
- Stock identification problems where there are multiple item numbers for the same stock descriptions, or different descriptions for the same stock.

10.4 Summary

The perpetual inventory as a database

Electronic databases ensure the fast and efficient storage and retrieval of inventory information. Modern perpetual inventory systems are essentially a database with a user interface and report-generating facilities. Perpetual inventory systems store transactions and link this information with look-up tables to build inventory tables that list all stock movements for any required period of time. In so doing, the perpetual stock can be generated and reviewed as required.

11: Inventory data fields

The term 'inventory data field' can refer either to a column of information within a database table, or to an individual data cell within a table column. To avoid confusion, here 'inventory data field' will refer exclusively to a table column.

While there are many fields that can be included and linked to an inventory item, the minimum are those that describe the stock, its quantity, location and value. Additional fields are only limited by the insights that they can bring the enterprise. Fields commonly used to support the stock-on-hand are shrinkage, period usage, re-order lead-time, safety margin, and recommended minimum and maximum stock levels. Following are some of the more common inventory database fields.

11.1 Item

In order to define different items within an inventory without actually seeing the items themselves, it is necessary to have information which describes each item. There are numerous ways in which this can be done, including specific descriptions, unique item numbers or even by recording the exact physical dimensions of a particular item.

Stock description

Stock description refers to the words used to name each item of stock. Stock descriptors should be standardized and used consistently.

Standardization involves defining the type and length of descriptor fields. By standardizing the number and length of fields, more consistent data entry can be achieved. This facilitates user learning and meaning and ensures faster and easy search times.

Consistency can be enforced by restricting the number of people that can enter stock descriptors and set rules about using capitals, abbreviations and such. Also, managers should insist on using certain descriptors and their placement consistently.

Stock properties

Increasingly item height, length, width and weight fields are recorded within the inventory. Dimensions are used by merchandising systems to calculate the area or volume consumed by each stock item. Weight is used in manufacture and distribution systems to track information such as shelf capacity and vehicle loading limits.

Given the current ease of taking digital photographs, many enterprises maintain images of each item of stock. The file name and location for each image is stored within the inventory. Images are used in merchandising systems to populate planograms. They are also essential for marketing, particularly for websites with shopping cart facilities.

Item number

It is not necessary for every single item to be numbered; however, a single and unique number for each item type is unambiguous, and ensures that an item is uniquely defined. There are many terms for the item number, including stock keeping unit (SKU), price look-up unit (PLU) or part number. While different names are used, they all refer to the same concept—a unique stock identifier.

Storing stock items under unique item numbers helps standardize their description and facilitates their correct and consistent use when purchased, manufactured, transferred or sold. Consequently, many enterprises choose to develop their own item numbering systems, which can usually be managed by their computer system.

11.2 Stock quantity

The quantity used to describe the stock may sound trivial, but it is an important part of the inventory record. The quantity used to measure stock may vary both between and within enterprises. In some cases it is even possible for the same item to be measured using different quantities in different situations.

Unit of quantity

At its simplest, stock should be counted in whole units; however, in some circumstances stock may need to be counted in partial units to one or more decimal places. For instance in a hotel or bar, high-value liquor is bought by the bottle, but is sold at the bar in 'nips' or 'shots' and may be counted in tenths.

An enterprise might also wish to count the same item in different quantities at different points along its supply chain. For example, it may handle a fast selling item in units of hundreds in their warehouses and sell the same item in singles at their retail outlets. This could mean that a single item has multiple quantity fields to express the stock quantity on hand in different ways. Alternatively, the same item may have multiple item numbers, each representing a different standard number of units. For instance, a product might have one item number when sold by the case, and another when sold by the piece. In the retail trade these are sometimes known as 'case/each', 'parent/child' or 'momma/baby' items.

Unit of measure

Often stock quantities must be stored in units of measure such as length, weight or area. These are often easily confused, causing major stock quantity errors. For instance, imagine a wholesaler who measures floor boards in area (length by width), but measures other timber such as railing only by length. This may be helpful to customers when purchasing these goods, however, employees could confuse the two and record board by length and not area. If different units of measure are applied within the same enterprise, care must be taken to prevent inventory record inaccuracy.

11.3 Location

Critical to an understanding of stock is its location. If stock is not tracked and consequently lost, it may take a stock count before it is found again. This has the potential to result in missed deadlines, lost sales, reduced cash flow (on replacement stock) and reduced storage space.

Location numbers

Location systems used in warehouses differ markedly from those in a retail setting. Typically, within a warehouse—particularly one that is very large—a unique bin location is applied to each area where stock is stored so that it may easily be found.

A common location numbering system is to allocate alternating alphabetical letters and Arabic numbers to each level of the location description as shown in Figure 11.1. Such location numbers should be unique.

1	A	08	D	01
Site	Aisle	Bay	Shelf	Position

Figure 11.1: Sample location number.

Each item can either be stored in its own unique location, in multiple locations, or even in a dynamic system with multiple items in multiple overlapping locations. Such dynamic systems need integrated computer systems to be managed effectively.

Historically, retail location systems have been simpler and did not specify detail beyond the aisle or gondola level. However, this is changing. Increasingly retailers are using merchandising systems to develop planograms and record stock location at a fixture, shelf and facing level.

11.4 Stock price or value

Within the inventory database it is possible to have multiple fields which describe an item's value. When using an inventory to determine the stock value for each item number, the quantity is multiplied by its corresponding price and summed for all items. The accuracy of the price is just as important as the accuracy of the stock quantity and, indeed, it is only possible to generate a meaningful valuation when both the quantity and price are correct.

Different valuation methods will be used depending on the purpose of the valuation. The last purchase price is used to calculate the market value of stock. This is done when stock needs to be insured, or when a business is being sold. Specific cost price, first in, first out (FIFO), last in, first out (LIFO) and average price are all different methods used in financial valuations.

An enterprise may choose any of these methods to value its stock, but the method must be used consistently during any accounting period (typically 12 months). Often the decision is based on the nature of the enterprise (retail, warehousing, etc.), its accounting policies, and the type of inventory management system it chooses.

11.5 Setting stock levels

The most basic perpetual inventory contains information relating to an item, its quantity, location and value. However, other fields such as purchases, sales, lead-time and minimum and maximum stock quantities can also be included in a database. These are necessary in order to optimize stock levels given supply and demand over time.

Lead-time

The item lead-time refers to the amount of time it takes for stock to be manufactured or sourced from suppliers after it is ordered. The lead-time of different items—both within and between industries—varies greatly, and can be expressed in working days, weeks or as a percentage of a period such as a week or month.

Stock usage and stock safety margins

Consider a retailer who estimates the average number of sales per week for an item and automatically orders more if the item's stock-on-hand drops below a certain level.

Monitoring stock usage based on past sales and calculating minimum safe stock levels based on re-order times is prudent, especially for critical items with long sourcing cycles, high manufacture costs or high margins. This strategy avoids unexpected out-of-stocks, missed orders and disappointed customers. However, stock usage models require detailed analyses of past sales and meaningful forecasting models if they are to be reliable.

Optimal order quantity

The optimal order quantity describes the most efficient quantity to be purchased from a supplier, given the following factors: stock usage, order lead-time, any relevant bulk buying discounts or minimum order quantities, and transportation costs. Bulk buying discounts must be relevant, because it could be either commercially non-viable for an enterprise to purchase too large an order, or the costs of storing the stock for an excessively long time could outweigh the benefits of the bulk discount.

Minimum stock-on-hand quantity

Using these field concepts it is possible to calculate the minimum stock level or re-order point (ROP). This refers to the lowest stock-on-hand quantity an enterprise should have in order to prevent a stock run-out. It must take into account three things: the predicted usage, the lead-time and a safety margin.

$$\text{safety stock} = \text{ROP} \times \text{safety margin}$$

$$\text{safe ROP} = \text{ROP} + \text{safety stock}$$

Consider an item with a usage of 50 units per week, a re-order time of 14% (1 day) and safety stock margin of 10%. This reflects a relatively reliable, easy-to-order product. The ROP is $50 \times 14\% = 7$, with $10\% \times 7 = 0.7$ added for a safety stock margin, giving 7.7 and rounded up to give a safe ROP of 8 units. In other words, when the stock-on-hand quantity reaches 8 units, the stock should be re-ordered at the optimal quantity.

Only fast-moving or high-spoilage items are ordered daily but the calculations and principles remain the same for whatever usage, re-order times and safety stock margins specified. Also note that the theoretical minimum stock-on-hand quantity for this item is 1 unit: 1 day's usage past the safe ROP before the next order has arrived (or simply the safety margin), and that the maximum quantity is 15 units, which corresponds to the safe ROP plus 1 day of unused demand.

11.6 Summary

Database tables and fields

The perpetual inventory hosted on a computer system consists of a database with many tables. Each table is made up of data fields (columns) that list the essential inventory information including item number, quantity, location and pricing. This and other modeling data (like re-order rates and safety margins) can be used to calculate more insightful fields. The resulting information can be used to assist mangers to efficiently manage stock levels by ensuring they have enough stock-on-hand to meet customer demand, while at the same time limiting stock holding costs.

12: Inventory data capture

The increasing use of the computer and large volumes of data made it necessary to capture item numbers and related inventory information in an electronic format quickly and accurately.

12.1 Automated data entry technology

Punch card technology was first invented for use with mechanical devices like textile machines and pianos several hundred years ago. Between 1900 and 1950 punch cards were used for data entry and storage for all institutional computing. However, by the 1960s punch card data storage was gradually replaced by magnetic tape.

In the 1950s, faced with increasing numbers of checks to process, the banking industry introduced printable fonts that could be read by people and—when printed using magnetic sensitive ink—could be read by a computer. This technology is still used on the bottom of checks today.

12.2 Barcodes

The best known printed computer readable data entry format, used widely to help manage inventories, must be the humble barcode. The first US patent for a barcode product was issued to inventors Woodland and Silver in 1952.

A modern barcode consists of a pattern of dark lines on a contrasting white background. Different systems of barcode patterns are called 'symbologies'. Some commonly used symbologies are Code 39,

Plessey, MSI and Interleaved 2 of 5. EAN numbers for instance, use Code 39 (see Figure 12.1).

Figure 12.1: Sample one-dimensional barcode (using Code 39 symbology).

While barcode scanning computer devices can read characters far more reliably than people, they can still misread. To improve reliability symbologies utilize extra digits that provide automatic data integrity checking.

Barcodes are cheap to produce, but one-dimensional symbologies (with one line of bars) are limited in the amount of information they can store in a reasonable space, usually either 8 or 13, but sometimes up to 20 characters. Two-dimensional barcodes (with multiple lines) are a solution to this problem, and can contain thousands of characters.[14] Figure 12.2 shows an example of a two-dimensional barcode.

Figure 12.2: Sample two-dimensional barcode.

In order to avoid duplicate item numbers across different enterprises a number of product numbering systems and conventions have been established. The 12-digit UPC, and 8-digit UPC-E conventions were established during the 1970s for retail trade in the US. Shortly afterwards, Europe introduced its own 13-digit European Article Number (EAN-13) and 8-digit EAN-8 systems. The International Standard Book Number (ISBN) is another well-known system used for cataloguing books, which can be read by EAN barcode-reading equipment.

Both UPC and EAN numbering systems now come under the Global Trade Item Numbers (GTIN) system. The GTIN system, apart from regulating readability and appearance of different systems, has also introduced a 14-digit barcode to compensate for the shrinking availability of unique item numbers.

The use of secure and standardized barcodes across the world has improved stock logistic processes for all stakeholders. Different stock items are now unlikely to have the same barcodes and stock can be more reliably tracked back to its source country and manufacturer. Printing, labeling and database management costs are also saved by using shared numbers.

The use of a global system has solved many, but not all issues. For example, UPC and EAN numbers must be purchased, creating additional unnecessary costs for an enterprise, especially if the stock is never to be sold in a retail setting. Consequently, universal compliance is still an issue.

12.3 Barcode readers

There are various barcode-reading technologies installed into a wide variety of computer platforms. Wand or pen barcode readers consist of a single small light source that the user swipes across a barcode. Charge-coupled device (CCD) readers are similar and consist of an array of photodiodes. They convert the ambient light from the barcode into a voltage. Microprocessors interpret the voltage pattern to ascertain the barcode.

Laser barcodes project a laser light onto an oscillating mirror or a rotating prism. A photodiode detects the reflected light, converts it to an electric waveform and analyzes the underlying barcode. Lastly, modern barcode readers use digital camera technology to capture an image of the barcode. Digital image processing techniques decode the barcode and interpret it.

Although performance varies depending on the quality of the barcode and the environment, most barcode-reading technologies reliably read and store barcodes from a range of angles and up to several feet away in less than a second.

12.4 Handheld devices

Since barcode readers are suited to automated data capture they are lined or installed in a range of computer platforms. Commercially they are used in retail check-outs, freight and logistics enterprises, libraries and many other enterprises.

Barcode readers installed in small handheld devices have a myriad of names including portable data terminals (PDTs), portable data entry devices (PDEs), data capture units, scanners, and so on. Essentially, they are all small, handheld portable computers with a built-in barcode reader, screen, central processors, electronic memory, data entry keyboard, communication ports, and battery. They are widely used in data capture applications like stock picking, ordering and counting.

Depending on their hardware design, handheld devices can communicate with other computer devices in several ways. Older technology uses serial port cable connection, whereas more modern devices use USB connection, flash memory cards, infra-red or bluetooth technology. Data is stored in a file and transferred in a batch to another device. In order for two devices to communicate they must be connected by cable, physically pass memory cards or be close enough to make a connection and pass data files.

Some handheld devices also support radio frequency (RF) technology where data can be transferred using WiFi, or other radio frequency data transfer protocols. While batch communication requires physical connection or proximity of devices, RF technology allows the convenient and automated data transfer over greater distance (over 300 ft or 100 m). Increasingly, enterprise applications are moving away from batch data transfer towards RF data transfer. Figure 12.3 shows some commonly manufactured handheld devices, including an older model using a barcode reading wand, a pistol grip model, a handheld device and a hip worn unit.

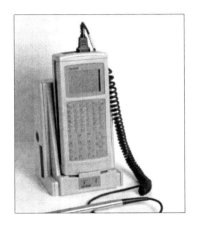

Figure 12.3: Examples of handheld devices.

12.5 RFID tags

Radio frequency identification (RFID) tags are electronic devices that store data in an electronic format and can receive and transfer that data using radio frequencies to other electronic devices. Figure 12.4 provides a sample of a passive RFID tag. Whereas a barcode is an inert printed label and can only be read by a reader that traverses the barcode, an RFID tag is a dynamic electronic device. It can store much more information than one-dimensional barcodes and can be read automatically from various distances, even without a direct line of sight.

Figure 12.4: Example of a passive RFID tag.

RFID tags typically consist of a micro chip that stores and controls the data and an antenna that is used to receive and transmit the data. There are two common designs: active devices that have their own battery power source, and passive devices that can only transmit when they are 'scanned'.

RFID tags are becoming increasingly cheaper, and at the time of writing, depending on the type and volume, passive devices can be produced for under US$0.20 each.[15] Programmed tags are embedded into printed labels with readable text for convenience, allowing them to be read by both RF readers and people. Unique numbers can be programmed and stored in each stock item, making feasible stock tracking at an item level. The unique number may consist of a fixed component that represents the item number and a variable component that is a unique number for every single unit. Tags can be used at an item level, box or pallet level and passed between manufacturer, distributor and retailer, making stock tracking more transparent and flexible. Finally, the information contained within RFID tags can be encrypted and made secure so that only particular devices can read them. Automated devices can be used to read and count hundreds of individual items in seconds, making stock counting fast and independent of people.

Unfortunately there are still a number of issues associated with the reliability and security of RFID tags. For instance, some metals and liquids absorb and reduce RFID signal strength while other devices that transmit radio frequencies can interfere with RFID signals. Also a small proportion of tags may be faulty (1–2%).[16] While their cost is ever decreasing, compared to a printed barcode, they are still expensive.

In regard to the stock count, marking stock with RFID tags is very appealing. In principle, a stock counter need only wave an RFID reading device over the stock to count and record it all in seconds. Counters need not handle the stock to physically count it. However, care must be taken to ensure that each item of stock is actually paired to an RFID tag. Just reading an RFID tag does not prove it is either physically attached to stock or represents the stock that it is attached to.

Also, because the device can read through walls, around corners and such, it is difficult to know the exact location and items of stock counted. Lastly, to prevent the same item being counted twice, each RFID tag must store a unique number or be temporarily deactivated after it has been read. Unique RFID item numbers create huge databases and require greater computer resources to manage them.

Only once these issues have been addressed is it likely that RFID tags will emerge as the preferred technology to barcodes.

12.5 Summary

The information technology revolution has led to the capture of large volumes of data quickly and accurately.

Barcodes have revolutionized the representation and capture of item numbers in manufacture, distribution and retail. The printed barcode is cheap and accessible and can be read by a range of barcode readers installed with computers.

RFID tags are a relatively recent development. They are growing cheaper and are increasingly used in distribution to track pallets and larger stock items. They have the potential to revolutionize stock counting and inventory management, but practical issues remain that currently limit their application.

III: Notes

1   Orlicky, Joseph. *Material Requirements Planning: The new way of life in production and inventory management.* New York: McGraw Hill, 1975.

2   Muller, Max. *Essentials of Inventory Management.* New York: American Management Association, 2003, p. 130.

3   Plossl, George. *Orlicky's Material Requirements Planning.* New York: McGraw Hill, 1994.

4   Muller, p. 137.

5   McKinnon, A.C., Mendes, D. and Nababteh, M. In-store logistics: An analysis of on-shelf availability and stockout responses for three product groups. *Journal of Logistics: Research and Applications*, vol. 10, no. 3, 2003, pp. 251–68.

6   Bezawada, Ram, et al. Cross category effects of aisle and display placements: A spacial modeling approach and insights. *Journal of Marketing*, vol. 73, 2009.

7   Doherty, Katherine. Toasting to success. *Food Logistics*, 2008, pp. 24–7.

8   Muller, p. 138.

9   Klaus, Helmut, Rosemann, Michael and Gable, Guy. What is ERP? *Information Systems Frontiers*, vol. 2, no. 2, pp. 141–62.

10   Ross, Jeanne W. and Vitale, Michael R. The ERP revolution: Surviving vs. thriving. *Information Systems Frontiers,* vol. 2, no. 2, 2000.

11   Klaus, Rosemann and Gable.

12   Strong, Diane and Volkoff, Olga. A roadmap for enterprise system implementation. *Computer*, vol. 37, no. 6, 2004, pp. 22–9.

13   Klaus, Rosemann and Gable, p. 142.

14   White, Gareth R.T., et al. A comparison of barcoding and RFID technologies in practice. *Journal of Information, Information Technology, and Organizations*, vol. 2, 2007, p. 122.

15   Smith, Jasmine. Bang for your buck? RFID technology examined. *Inside Retailing Magazine*. Oct.–Nov. 2008, pp. 30–2.

16   White et al., p. 122.

PART IV: INVENTORY ACCURACY

13: Defining accuracy

In this section inventory accuracy and error are defined. The means by which inventories are compared and accuracy measured is also discussed.

One purpose of the inventory is to provide a list that represents physical stock. At the very least it will detail the stock identifier, location and quantity; in other words 'what, where and how many'.

Since the inventory is a representation of stock, its detail and accuracy will vary depending on how it is generated. Common inventory sources include:

- a perpetual inventory generated using a computer system that combines all stock sales, purchases and transfers over time
- a stock count inventory generated by completing a physical count of the stock
- other inventory records such as invoice or delivery records from an independent source such as a supplier, manufacturer or inventory service provider.

In practice, an inventory may be imperfect. That is, it may not correctly reflect the physical stock that it seeks to represent. Imagine any typical busy enterprise, with hundreds of stock transactions each day. Stock picking, purchase and sales mistakes, incorrect period cut-offs or willful theft and fraud may all lead to inconsistencies between the perpetual inventory and the physical stock on the shelf. Ultimately an inaccurate inventory can decrease enterprise profits by causing stock outages, lost sales and disguising stock loss.

So, how is inventory accuracy determined? As yet there is no commercial automated stock counting technology. People must still physically verify and count the stock on the shelf from time to time to verify that it exists. A stock count may merely confirm one's memory, establish a new inventory or verify a perpetual inventory. Regardless, all enterprises are forced to use the stock count as a means to verify their perpetual or other types of inventories.

If the stock is tidy and well prepared, counters are alert and motivated, and the count process is thorough and reliable, the stock count has its best chance at generating an accurate stock inventory. That is, the stock count will then provide a true representation of the underlying stock levels. Equally, if counters are careless, the stock preparation is poor and period-end cut-offs are not definitive, the stock count accuracy is likely be very low.

So, how accurate is the stock count? Unfortunately, there is no calibrated inventory device that measures its accuracy. At best, all measures of inventory accuracy merely compare two or more inventory counts for each stock item, followed by some analysis of any discrepancies. The two comparative inventories can be from any source; but two or more stock counts, or a stock count and a perpetual inventory, are commonly paired.

If the item number and quantity match in each inventory, the item is thought to be accurate and reflects the true physical stock level. Admittedly, there is a small chance that even if both inventories agree, they are still wrong. When two inventories disagree, without recounting the item, one cannot know in which inventory the error lies; indeed it might even be in both. The nature of inventory accuracy and the probability of these different events are considered in more detail below.

13.1 Inventory error

Inventory error is defined as any quantity difference greater than a predetermined tolerance between two counts of the same item in the same location. An item tolerance could be any commercial discrepancy the enterprise deems acceptable. It might be a discrepancy of units, value or a proportion.[1,2]

Drawing on this definition, the number of discrepant items are counted and expressed relative to the number of all items. This ratio defines error as a proportion between 0 and 1. Furthermore, inventory accuracy can be defined as 1 minus the proportion of error (i.e. accuracy = 1 – error).

To clarify this definition, consider the fictitious enterprise data in Figure 13.1. For simplicity, the enterprise has only 10 items in one location. Each item of stock is numbered using a unique item number and cost price. Item 1001, for instance, has a perpetual inventory record of 11, whereas a stock count conducted of this item observed a quantity of 10.

Now consider the measure of inventory error using 3 different accuracy tolerances. In the first case the tolerance is any discrepancy between the inventory record quantity and the stock count quantity. That is, any difference between the two inventory records that exceeds the tolerance of 0% variance is deemed to be an error. Counting the total number of discrepancies over all items reveals 4 errors. These 4 errors can be expressed as a percentage of the total number of items where 4 / 10 × 100 = 40% error. In other words, inventory error is 40% and conversely inventory accuracy is the difference, 100% – 40% = 60%.

In the second case, the tolerance is defined as any quantity variance greater than ±5% of the inventory quantity. For instance, item number 1001, with a perpetual record of 11 and stock count of 10, has a difference of 1. One, as a percentage of the perpetual record, is 111, or 9%. Since 9% is greater than 5%, the item number tolerance has been exceeded and the item is deemed to be in error. Using this choice of tolerance, there are 3 items in error for 10 item numbers and therefore inventory error is 30% and inventory accuracy is the balance, at 70%.

Item #	Cost price	Perpet. qty	SOH qty	Qty var.	% var.	$ var.	Tolerance Zero qty	5% qty	$25 var.
1001	$20.00	11	10	1	9	$20.00	x	x	
1002	$5.50	20	20	0	0	$–			
1003	$8.11	16	16	0	0	$–			
1004	$2.46	232	226	6	3	$14.76	x		
1005	$0.34	9,924	11,169	–1,245	–13	–$423.30	x	x	x
1006	$1.21	454	454	0	0	$–			
1007	$36.35	45	45	0	0	$–			
1008	$0.50	3,582	3,800	–218	–6	–$109.00	x	x	x
1009	$1.21	454	454	0	0	$–			
1010	$45.00	65	65	0	0	$–			
Totals							**4**	**3**	**2**

Figure 13.1: Simple two-inventory comparison with various variance tolerances.

In the third case, the tolerance is any absolute quantity variance multiplied by the cost price, greater than a preset value of $25. For instance, item number 1005, with a cost price of $0.34 has a variance of 1245 units.

Thirty-four cents multiplied by –1245 is –$423.30. Since this sum is less than the ± $25 tolerance, there is an inventory error. Using this method there are 2 items in error for 10 item numbers and the inventory error is 20%. That is, the inventory accuracy is 80%.

Choosing tolerances

Using selective tolerances allows the enterprise to be pragmatic and adjust the measure of inventory accuracy to suit the commercial circumstance in which the stock is used. Tolerances can be based on any formula, be it differences of quantity, value, or proportion. They can be used for simple inquiries into stock levels or complex modeling of supply and demand. They can also be asymmetric where positive discrepancies are weighted differently from negative discrepancies.

In theory, tolerances can be set for each individual item, but this is time-consuming and difficult to justify. More commonly, general tolerances are applied to specific stock categories depending on typical unit size and valuation. These may be changed over time if required, and even during seasonal peaks and troughs.

Stock counts in the military, for example, require that dangerous and mission-critical items (like weapons and ammunition) have a zero stock loss tolerance, regardless of unit value. Alternatively, for items with a low value, high use and short re-order time—like ration packs—a modest tolerance is accepted.

Establishing and maintaining individual tolerances is a lot of work, where each must be thoughtfully reviewed, implemented and monitored. In practice, some enterprises simply use a blanket tolerance of ±5% of stock quantity or a standard stock value discrepancy like $100. For instance, if an item count differs from the stock-on-hand inventory by more than ±5%, the item is considered to be an error.

Specifying a location

Like an accuracy tolerance, the location can be measured at any level, depending on the requirement of the enterprise.

In a manufacturing or distribution environment, where stock may be stored in randomly assigned bins, the exact stock location at a row and shelf level is essential. Merely knowing that stock is on-site is not adequate. It must be possible to find the stock quickly and easily, using its inventory location reference or 'bin number'.

Historically, many retailers only recorded stock location at a shop level. Even though perpetual stock systems support recording stock with multiple locations within a store, the effort to record and maintain such detail was thought to outweigh its benefits. However, this thinking is changing.

Modern retailers increasingly seek to standardize and optimize the volume and placement of stock within their stores. Merchandising stock systems provide recommended stock locations down to the store, fixture, shelf and facing level. During stock counts, for each item the store, fixture, shelf and facing will be recorded, along with the stock quantity. This detail can then be compared to the planogram and any discrepancies corrected.

Item #	Location	Qty	Stock count	Tolerance ±0%	Tolerance pass/fail
1003	–	3000	3000	0	–
Total		3000	3000	0	–

Figure 13.2: Inventory error measurement for one item with one location.

Item #	Location	Inventory record	Stock count qty	Tolerance ±0%	Tolerance pass/fail
1003	A003	1000	1000	0	–
1003	A004	1000	900	–100	x
1003	A005	1000	1100	100	x
Total		3000	3000	0	2

Figure 13.3: Inventory error measurement for one item with three locations.

Location can be included in any measure of inventory accuracy as long as it is collected in both inventories. Figures 13.2 and 13.3 provide simple examples to illustrate. In Figure 13.2, item 1003 exists in only one location. The inventory record has 3000 items and so too does the stock count. Accordingly there is no discrepancy between the two items and no error is recorded.

Figure 13.3 shows item 1003 with three locations recorded in the perpetual and stock count inventories. In the example, the item number and location are recorded and compared when determining the inventory error. Item and location number 1003-A003 balances, but 1003-A004 has a shortage of 100 units and is in error.

Similarly, item 1003-A005 has a surplus of 100 units and is also in error.

The sum of these variances (+100 and –100) for item 1003 cancels out, so at the store level, there is no quantity shortfall. However, the quantity is incorrect in two locations and therefore two item-level errors are recorded. Adding location detail increased the frequency of inventory errors from zero to two.

There is a trend toward recording stock with ever more item detail, including a hierarchy of locations. Separating the same item into multiple locations is like adding additional unique items. This detail adds complexity to the inventory and requires extra effort to maintain and report accurately. Similar stock is easily confused, incorrectly picked and placed in an alternate location. During a stock count, each item must be counted and reconciled in its location. A useful measure of inventory accuracy must ensure both a realistic commercial accuracy tolerance and practical item location detail.

13.2 Inventory deviation

Other techniques used to compare two or more inventories do not actually measure the number of item errors as a proportion of the total number of items. Instead they compare the total magnitude of differences for all items. For this reason it is preferable to call them measures of 'inventory deviation' rather than measures of 'inventory error'. Two such methods are valuation deviation and absolute quantity deviation. These are considered below.

Valuation deviation

The valuation deviation is simply the difference between two inventory stock valuations for the same items. It can be calculated by determining the total valuation for each inventory and deducting one from the other, or it can be calculated by obtaining the valuation difference for each item and summing all differences.

Interest in the stock valuation deviation is hardly surprising given that this was the original purpose of the inventory. Stock constitutes a valuable asset and all enterprise stakeholders have an interest in its worth. If a stock count inventory valuation is close to its perpetual inventory valuation, it is tempting to assume that the comparative inventories at an item level are accurate.

Of course, knowing the valuation for each inventory is essential, but it may easily hide an inaccurate inventory at the item, location and quantity level. Large item-level discrepancies may cancel each other out when summed, providing a valuation that approximately balances, but is misleading.

To illustrate, Figure 13.4 presents a valuation table by department for a small grocery store. The valuation deviation for each department is summed. Note that some department valuations balance well (within 1%) and others have major discrepancies (up to 26%). However, summing all departments, the valuation balances (within 1%).

Category	Perpetual inventory valuation	Stock count inventory valuation	Deviation in $	Deviation %
Grocery	$15,123.00	$16,244.00	$1,121.00	7
Cereal	$2,300.00	$2,275.00	−$25.00	−1
Clothing	$6,894.00	$5,846.00	−$1,048.00	−15
Health	$19,623.22	$18,456.98	−$1,166.24	−0.6
Variety	$5,462.35	$5,948.37	$ 486.02	9
Deli	$4,523.00	$4,856.00	$ 333.00	7
Check-out	$1,217.34	$895.62	−$ 321.72	−26
Total	**$55,142.91**	**$54,521.97**	**−$ 620.94**	**−1**

Figure 13.4: Sample inventory valuation deviation.

Unlike the proportion of error used to measure perpetual stock accuracy, the valuation deviation indicates the financial impact of a stock discrepancy on the enterprise. Interestingly, for most enterprises, especially in the retail sector, the stock count valuation will invariably be a little lower than the perpetual stock value.

This difference is usually due to shrinkage, particularly theft. By contrast, sometimes in a supply chain enterprise, the stock count valuation is higher than the perpetual stock value because stock lost in another location that was previously written-off is found during the stock count.

While a measure of inventory error at the item level may indicate problems with the management of the physical stock and the efficiencies in an enterprise, the valuation deviation indicates whether such problems are of financial significance.

Quantity deviation

Some enterprises measure the accuracy of their perpetual stock inventory by considering the magnitude of quantity discrepancies relative to a stock count inventory. Consider an enterprise with a stock holding of 10 items. Figure 13.5 compares two inventories of these 10 stock items.

The sum of the quantity deviation is 112. Expressed as a percentage relative to the total volume of items in the perpetual inventory provides a total deviation of $112 / 5000 \times 100 = 2.2\%$. There may still be large positive and negative quantity discrepancies between items, however. Summing these terms without adjusting signs can produce a small total discrepancy. To avoid this effect, many enterprises choose to ignore the arithmetic sign of each discrepancy and sum the absolute quantity discrepancy. Using this approach in the example, the absolute quantity deviation becomes 324. Expressed as a percentage relative to the total of the perpetual inventory provides total deviation of $324 / 5000 \times 100 = 6.5\%$.

Note that deviation measures, such as quantity and value, indicate the magnitude of the discrepancies between inventories and not the number of errors. For this reason they are called measures of deviation, difference or variance, and not measures of error.

Item	Perpetual inventory	Stock count	Qty dev.	Abs. qty dev.
1001	100	99	−1	1
1002	20	20	0	0
1003	16	16	0	0
1004	232	132	−100	100
1005	32	29	−3	3
1006	454	454	0	0
1007	45	45	0	0
1008	3,582	3,800	218	218
1009	454	452	−2	2
1010	65	65	0	0
Total	**5,000**	**5,112**	**112**	**324**
Qty deviation 112 / 5000 × 100 = 2.2%				
Abs qty dev. 324 / 5000 × 100 = 6.5%.				

Figure 13.5: Quantity deviation comparisons for two inventories.

Historically, quantity deviation was often used by enterprises that did not report their inventory at an item level, or where all of the prices of items were similar. The net quantity deviation simply indicated the absolute magnitude of quantity differences for all items.

13.3 Practical issues

To measure an inventory's accuracy, each item in its location must be compared to another inventory with the same location and item. Any item with a quantity discrepancy greater than a predefined tolerance is defined as an error.

The number of discrepancies (or errors) is expressed as a proportion of the total number of inventory items. The number of balanced items can also be expressed as a proportion of the total number of inventory items (accuracy). Thus, the sum of accurate items and items in error will equal the total inventory items. This definition expresses accuracy and error relative to each other as proportions of one, or, if expressed as a percentage, between zero and 100%.

Since accuracy and error are relative proportions, they can also be considered in terms of probability theory. For instance, an error rate of 5% can be expressed as a 0.05 probability that any inventory item will be in error. Accordingly, if 20 items are randomly checked, we would expect one of them to be in error.

Deviation measures, such as quantity and value, indicate the magnitude of discrepancies between inventories and not the number of errors. Deviation measures of accuracy have no upper range. For example, given an item stock count of 10 and an expected perpetual stock quantity of 1, the quantity deviation is 9 (= 10 − 1). Expressed as a percentage this is 900% (9 / 1 × 100 = 900%) greater than the expected quantity. The error is measured using relative units and can be infinitely large, which may not be very helpful.

Using a tolerance to define the level of discrepancy gives this definition of error great flexibility. A range of tolerance criteria can be considered and are not limited to one criterion at a time. For example, quantity, value and percentage tolerances can all be used concurrently in the same measure of inventory accuracy.

Naturally, any reference to a level of accuracy should also stipulate what tolerances have been applied. Consider the difference between an accuracy rate of 99% with a 5% tolerance and an accuracy rate of 95% with a 0% tolerance. The former inventory may have many small undetected discrepancies between 1–5%; whereas the latter indicates that 1 in 20 items are in error, the magnitude of which could be anywhere between 1% and >1000%.

As with tolerances, deviation methods also weight the magnitude of any discrepancy, but only with respect to one variable at a time. This is still useful. Expressing the valuation discrepancy between an expected perpetual inventory and stock count inventory is still meaningful.

However, a deviation method does not indicate the number of items that created the deviations. A small discrepancy across 100 items could be equivalent to a large discrepancy across one item. Deviation measures can be swamped by either high-value items or large-quantity items. In the same way, huge deviations across only a few items with an error-based measure of accuracy can have their significance diluted by many accurate items, potentially of far less significance.

There is no agreed benchmark on the proportion of stock error that is acceptable. Standards vary widely depending on the industry, stock size and range and management requirements. However, widely cited figures seem to lie between 95% and 99% .[3]

13.4 Summary

Comparing inventories

An inventory is a representation of physical stock and may be imperfect. In order to determine its accuracy, it must be compared to another independent inventory with the same items at the same instant in time.

Defining error

Inventory error is defined as any quantity difference greater than a predetermined tolerance between two counts of the same item in the same location. An item tolerance may be any discrepancy deemed commercially practical and acceptable. It might be a discrepancy of stock item units, value, location or proportion.

Error tolerances

Any reference to a level of accuracy should also stipulate what tolerances have been applied. Tolerances are flexible and can be applied according to item characteristics such as category, value, priority and desirability.

Item number and location

There is a trend toward recording stock with ever more item detail, including a hierarchy of locations. Separating the same item into multiple locations is like adding unique items, increasing the size of the inventory. A unique item with one stock keeping unit is divided into more unique item numbers consisting of a single SKU plus each unique location. When measuring inventory accuracy, each item plus its location must be counted and reconciled. Any measure of inventory accuracy must consider a practical level of item location detail.

Defining deviation

Other techniques used to compare two or more inventories do not actually measure the number of item errors as a proportion of the total number of items, but rather as a proportion of the total volume or valuation of the stock. The valuation deviation is the difference between two inventory stock valuations for the same items. The quantity deviation is the sum of the quantity differences for each item. Deviation measures can be calculated using the signed differences or the more conservative (larger) absolute differences.

Error versus deviation

Since accuracy and error are relative proportions between one and zero, they can be expressed as a probability. For instance, an error rate of 5% can be expressed as a 0.05 probability that any inventory item will be in error. Deviation measures, such as quantity and value, indicate the magnitude of discrepancy between inventories and not the number of errors. Deviation measures of accuracy have no upper range.

14: Comparing inventories

14.1 Calibration concepts

In the sciences, devices and methods have been invented and developed to measure the natural world. Simple examples are scales that measure weight in kilograms, tape measures that define length in meters, and thermometers that measure temperature in Celsius.[4]

Many measures and units commonly used in everyday commerce and science are described by the International System of Units. Abbreviated SI from the French, 'Le Systeme International d'Unites'. This system is used throughout the world, except in just three countries: Liberia, the United States and Myanmar.

Figure 14.1: International Prototype Kilogram.

Most measurement devices are calibrated using independently objective or repeatable processes. For example the point at which water boils is the calibration reference for 100°C and freezing water is the reference for 0°C. Weight is one of the few remaining SI units that still uses an artifact as its reference. All weight measuring scales in the world are calibrated from one of several 1 kilogram cylinders of platinum-iridium. The original is stored in Sèvres, France and is called the International Prototype Kilogram (IPK) (see Figure 14.1).

Even more complex concepts are the subject of measurement. Intelligence Quotient (IQ) tests seek to measure intelligence and economic surveys try to measure market sentiment. Difficulties emerge moving from the relatively objective scales used in the physical sciences, into the more subjective realm of psychology and economics. Measures that are affected by people's motivation and state of mind tend to generate greater variation and poorer reliability. Inventories are generated by people counting and processing stock. As such they are affected by human nature and error.

A stock count is a common procedure itself used to establish information about an inventory. So how is stock count accuracy established? The solution is to use an analogous method used to calibrate other devices. For example, in order to test if a balance scale is accurate something with a known weight, such as the IPK, is used as a reference. If the scale confirms the known weight the device is accurate, at least for the weight tested.

Similarly, to calibrate a stock count procedure, first an accurate inventory of a known and fixed stock must be established. This fixed inventory can then serve as a reference. A stock count would be conducted of the fixed stock and the resulting inventory compared to the reference inventory. If the stock count inventory agrees with the reference inventory, it is deemed accurate. These ideas are expanded in the following sections.

14.2 Accuracy versus precision

Two concepts commonly used in the science of measurement are accuracy and precision. The term 'accuracy' in this context refers to the closeness a measure has to its true value. By contrast, the term 'precision' refers to the repeatability or reliability of a measurement; that is, the likelihood that further measurements or calculations will demonstrate the same or similar results.[5]

A useful metaphor to explain these different concepts is that of a bullet hitting a target. The center of the target is easily identified and verified. It is a known and trusted reference or benchmark. Figure 14.2 shows two targets, one with many shots close to its center. This suggests high accuracy, but as they are spread widely over the target, the precision is low.

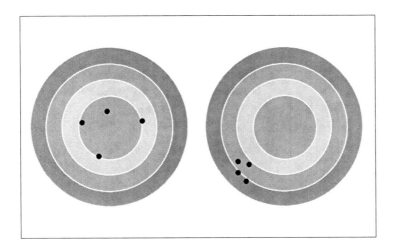

Figure 14.2: Two targets—the left shows accurate shots but imprecise, the right shows precise shots, but inaccurate.

The second image shows an alternative target with a higher level of precision since each strike is consistently near the other, but with low accuracy since none actually hit near the center. These concepts are independent of each other. A tight cluster of strikes around the center would demonstrate the ideal; high accuracy and high precision.

Note that while using this metaphor, it is easy to understand that accuracy and precision may also be improved if better equipment or methods are used. For instance, perhaps a better gun and more time taken to aim each shot will improve consistency (the precision) and proximity to the bull's eye (accuracy).

These concepts of accuracy and precision can also be explained using a statistical model. Figure 14.3 shows the relationship between a reference and a number of independent observations. The target's center is our reference. It is known and well-defined; hence it is shown as a straight line. The different shots fired at the target form a distribution. The spread of this distribution indicates the precision of the strikes and the average reflects the midpoint of all of the strikes. The distance between the average and the reference indicates the average accuracy, which is equivalent to the statistical concept of bias.

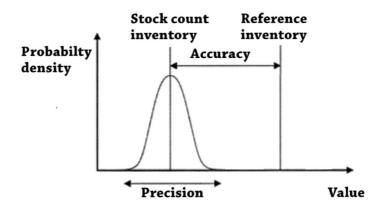

Exhibit 14.3: Accuracy and precision—statistical framework with fixed reference.

This statistical framework can also be applied to an inventory to determine if it is accurate. The reference would be a known and established inventory (analogous to the bull's eye). An inventory process such as a stock count could be conducted repeatedly to generate a sample of inventories (analogous to shots fired). The quantity deviation between items in each stock count inventory would reflect precision; that is, the reliability of the stock count procedure to generate the same inventory each time it was executed. The difference between the average item count in each inventory and the reference inventory would reflect the inventory's accuracy; that is the degree to which the stock count actually measured the stock of interest.

Unfortunately, there are considerable practical difficulties for an enterprise to apply this approach. Firstly, there is rarely a known and trusted reference inventory that is accurate and precise to compare with other inventories. Even if another independent inventory source is used, it too is likely to be imprecise. Figure 14.4 shows the distribution of two independent inventories, where both are imprecise and define accuracy differently. In this example, comparing averages for two inventory methods is like trying to shoot a target with a moving bull's eye. It is possible to hit the center, but as the center is poorly defined it is difficult to know when that happens.

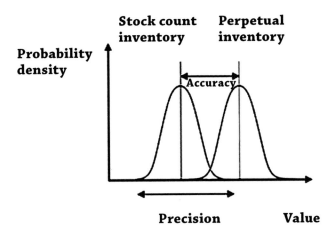

Figure 14.4: Accuracy and precision—statistical framework with variable reference.

A second problem faced by the enterprise when trying to determine inventory accuracy and precision is simply cost. In reality, repeatedly counting the same item and averaging the result to provide a statistical estimate of the likely physical quantity is very time-consuming, expensive and impractical. Most enterprises can only afford to conduct one stock count and not average many.

14.3 An imperfect ruler

Any stock inventory, be it a perpetual inventory or stock count inventory, will possess some error. Over time, human error, shrinkage, and counting mistakes will create differences between the inventory record and its corresponding physical stock. The inventory is an imperfect ruler that attempts to measure and represent physical stock and its attributes. Moreover, there is something of a chicken–egg paradox here, as it is not possible to determine the accuracy of any given inventory without comparing it to another imperfect inventory.

Comparing two imperfect measures

Consider a simple example to illustrate the problems of comparing two imperfect measures. Imagine two students, Jose and Jane, who each sit the same arithmetic test with 10 questions. The test results will be provided in a week by the examiner, but the students are wondering how well they performed beforehand. One way they can judge their performance is to compare their answers for each question. Where they have the same answer they assume that they are correct and where they differ they assume that they are both wrong.

When Jose and Jane compare their test questions they agree for eight questions and disagree for two. Of course, this does not mean that their final test score is eight out of ten. It depends on how many times they agreed with each other, yet still got the questions wrong. And even if they did agree with each other, which questions did they get right? Figure 14.5 presents three different result scenarios.

Exam responses		Scenario 1		Scenario 2		Scenario 3	
Question	True	Jose	Jane	Jose	Jane	Jose	Jane
1	A	A	A	A	A	A	A
2	B	B	B	B	B	B	B
3	C	C	C	C	C	C	C
4	D	D	D	D	D	D	D
5	C	C	C	C	C	C	C
6	D	D	D	D	D	D	D
7	A	A	A	A	A	A	A
8	B	B	B	B	B	B	B
9	A	A	C X	C X	B X	D X	D X
10	D	B X	D	C X	B X	C X	C X
Total true score		90%	90%	80%	80%	80%	80%
Agreement rate		80%		80%		100%	

Figure 14.5: Example comparison of test scores.

The first two columns refer to the question number and the teacher's correct or true answer (although in our story Jose and Jane are not privy to the true answer at the time they compared their results). In scenario 1, Jose and Jane had an agreement rate of 80%, but each achieved 90% accuracy relative to the teacher's true answers. This is because each only got one question wrong, but it was a different question for each. In scenario 2, Jose and Jane again had an agreement rate of 80%, but this time only achieved 80% accuracy each. This is because they each got exactly the same questions right and wrong. Lastly, in scenario 3, Jose and Jane obtain 100% agreement, but only achieve 80% accuracy. They always agreed, but they were both wrong on two questions.

The relationship between our two test scores and the unknown answers from the teacher are analogous to our experience with inventories. We know that there is a true stock that is observed on the shelf. We know it exists and we have indirect access to it, but we cannot prove its entire existence simply and instantaneously. At best, we can create an imperfect representation of it, such as an inventory. We know that the inventory is fallible and may contain some inaccuracies or error. Consequently, comparing two inventories, each with its own error, may lead to incorrect conclusions.

These concepts can be presented using a contingency diagram as is seen in Figure 14.6. Each circle represents an inventory or physical stock holding of items and their corresponding quantities at the same instant in time. Their degree of overlap with the true stock represents their agreement or the degree of accuracy. The non-overlapping areas represent items and quantities in disagreement or with error.

The 'true' labeled circle represents the true or actual physical stock level. In practice, we can never know exactly what stock there is at a point in time. This goes beyond the fundamental uncertainty of the external world proposed by philosophers like Descartes.[5] It is instead a practical issue of whether the count is being correctly performed; the stock could be on a different shelf, obscured behind other stock, or the stock counter could simply make a counting error. We can only represent stock using the imperfect inventory.

The 'stock count' circle represents a stock count. Assume it was systematically generated using sound procedures and motivated stock counters. The 'perpetual' circle represents another inventory. This could be generated by a perpetual stock system or even a second stock count.

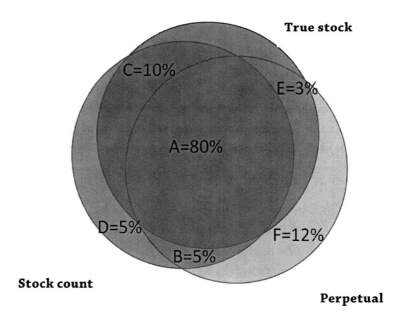

Figure 14.6: Contingency diagram showing the accuracy or concurrency of the physical stock and two inventories.

The merit of the contingency diagram is that the degree of overlap between the stock representations can be expressed as proportions or percentages. Consider the different schematic labels and percentages and what they indicate. (Note that in order to make the overlap between the circles clearer, the percentages do not exactly correspond to the size of the overlapping regions.)

The term 'accurate' is used here to indicate whether an inventory nominates the same quantity for an item as the true stock, and the term 'agreement' is used to indicate when two inventories nominate the same quantity relative to each other. Accordingly:

- all stock in A is in agreement and accurate
- all stock in B is in agreement but inaccurate
- C indicates stock count inventory items in disagreement but accurate
- D indicates stock count inventory items in disagreement and inaccurate
- E indicates perpetual inventory items in disagreement but accurate
- F indicates perpetual inventory items in disagreement and inaccurate
- the remaining true circle is left intentionally unnamed since it represents physical stock already present in other regions and cannot be defined in term of accuracy or agreement.

In practice, two inventories can be compared to determine their agreement and this used to approximate the accuracy of either inventory. A + B represents the overlap of the stock and perpetual inventories, and therefore their agreement rate.

While it is tempting to attribute disagreements to one of the two inventory sources, without further data, blame cannot be apportioned. In practice, acting conservatively it is assumed that any disagreement (C, D, E, or F) is cause for the item to be physically recounted.

Similarly, if the same item and quantity in each inventory concur it is assumed they are correct, but in reality they might both be wrong (B). Also, there will be items for which one inventory is correct and the other wrong (E and C). Nevertheless all such items require recounting.

14.4 Accuracy and duration trade-offs

When considering the accuracy and precision of an inventory it is also essential to consider its duration and cost. A perpetual or stock count inventory could be perfectly accurate if enough time and checking was allowed. Infinite time will arguably provide 100% accuracy with every single stock count. However, in the commercial world, an enterprise can never spend an indefinite amount of time measuring and verifying the physical stock.

Consider a simple example to highlight the relationship between item accuracy and time. A small experiment was conducted examining the counting accuracy and duration of a plastic bin containing 1000 washers.

A commercially calibrated scale was used to weigh a sample of 50 washers, and was then used to estimate the total quantity. Using this approach a quantity of 990 was nominated in about two minutes.

A number of people were then asked to count the contents of the bin as quickly as possible. Counters typically tipped the contents of the bin onto the floor, and quickly counted the number of washers as they slid them from an uncounted pile to a counted one. This took them on average about five minutes. The results obtained are presented in Figure 14.7. The average quantity was 999, with a range (or precision) from 991 to 1008.

Counter's nominated quantity				
Counter	1	2	3	4	5
Nominated qty	991	998	998	1000	1008

Figure 14.7: Individual counts of 1000 washers.

Finally, two stock counters were asked to count the quantity exactly by tipping the contents of the bin onto the floor, and arranging the washers into piles of 10, in rows of 10. The piles, once arranged, were then carefully inspected, and a total quantity of 1000 units was observed. This last process took 34 minutes. The average stock quantity and count duration for the three methods (weighing, quick counting and stacking before counting) are illustrated in Figure 14.8.

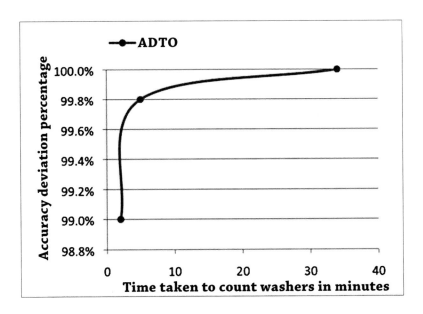

Figure 14.8: Illustration of the accuracy–duration trade-off when counting 1000 washers.

While reasonable levels of accuracy can be obtained quite quickly (in about two minutes using scales), a high or 'perfect' level of accuracy requires substantially—and usually prohibitively—more work (17 times longer). Thus stock count accuracy will improve if selected methods and more time are used. However, these alternatives come at a cost. Enterprise managers must be prepared to pay these costs to achieve the accuracy that they demand.

14.5 A fixed reference inventory

Although the stock count and perpetual inventories are used to measure and quantify physical stock, there is no way to calibrate their accuracy apart from comparing them. The precision of one may be no better than the other, and each may not represent the true stock.

It might be possible to generate a more accurate measure of stock, given more care and time. However, commercial enterprises cannot afford to cease trading, indefinitely freeze the stock and diligently count it. It is far too impractical and expensive. Only in a highly controlled experimental setting, where stock is fixed indefinitely, can a highly accurate inventory be established and used as a reference.

14.6 Summary

Independent measurement and calibration

Most measurement devices are calibrated using objective and repeatable processes. Inventories are generated by people counting and processing stock, and are affected by human nature and error. A stock count is a common procedure used to establish or verify another inventory, but unfortunately its accuracy cannot be easily independently determined.

Accuracy and precision

Two concepts commonly used in the science of measurement are accuracy and precision. The term 'accuracy' refers to the closeness a measure has to its true value; 'precision' refers to the repeatability or reliability of a measurement. The accuracy of a stock count, for instance, is the degree to which it truly represents the physical stock. Its reliability reflects any variations or differences in the accuracy with each stock count performed.

Contingency diagram

A contingency diagram can be used to represent one or more inventories and the physical stock that it measures. The degree of overlap with the true stock represents the degree of accuracy, whereas overlapping regions with other inventories represents the proportion of stock in agreement. The non-overlapping areas represent items and quantities in disagreement or with error.

A fixed reference

The difficulty faced when trying to determine the accuracy of an inventory is that there is no agreed reference. At best the physical stock must be repeatedly measured using similar methods and comparing them. Any method that seeks to determine inventory accuracy needs to be viable and achieved in a commercially affordable amount of time.

IV: Notes

1   Bryson, Marion, R. Physical inventory using sampling methods. *Applied Statistics*, vol. 9, no. 3, Nov. 1960, p. 180.

2   Brooks, Roger, B. and Wilson, Larry, W. *Inventory Record Accuracy*. Hoboken, New Jersey: John Wiley & Sons, 2007, p. 11.

3   Kutz, G. *Executive Guide: Best Practice in Achieving Consistent, Accurate Physical Counts of Inventory and Related Property*. Washington: United States General Accounting Office, 2002.

4   Fenna, Donald, *Oxford Dictionary of Weights, Measures and Units*, Oxford, UK, 2002.

5   Lohr, Sharon L. *Sampling: Design and Analysis*, Pacific Grove, USA, Brooks Cole Publishing, 1999.

6   For a discussion on Descartes, see Papineau, David and Selina, Howard, *Introducing Consciousness*, Icon Books, Cambridge, UK, 2000.

PART V: STOCK COUNT ACCURACY

15: A laboratory store

This section considers stock count accuracy in a laboratory store with static or fixed stock. Various counters were asked to complete a stock count of the store. Their results were examined in light of four stages of the stock count.

15.1 Four stock count stages

Regardless of its method or purpose, the stock count process can be separated into four distinct stages: preparing, counting, checking and sampling. The concept of four stock count stages helps the enterprise manager visualize the stock count process and accuracy over time.

Figure 15.1 represents these stock count stages. Time (equivalent to cost) is presented on the horizontal axis, whereas the vertical axis represents stock count accuracy.

The dotted horizontal line represents the level of accuracy of any pre-existing inventory (such as a perpetual inventory). The solid line represents the accuracy of a stock count inventory through its various stages.

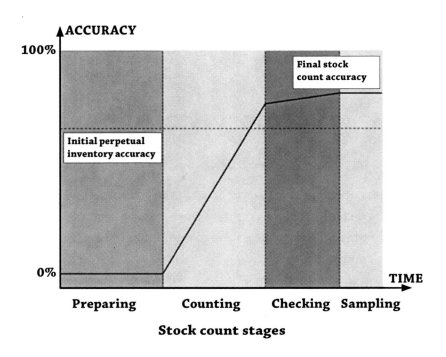

Figure 15.1: Stock count accuracy improvement across stages over time.

The preparing stage

Before the counting of any stock can begin, there must be the preparing stage. This is largely administrative and includes the organization of the stock and counters. It includes:

- neatly arranging the stock and ensuring it is accessible and labeled
- ceasing stock movements and verifying appropriate accounting cut-offs and quarantined areas
- ensuring adequate numbers of stock counters who are fully briefed, motivated and enthused
- ensuring enough fully-functioning handheld devices, including the correct validation file.

The act of preparing stock does not immediately benefit stock count accuracy or duration. However, good preparation will facilitate stock count accuracy during the counting stage. Well-prepared areas are likely to take less time and be more easily and accurately counted.

The counting stage

The counting stage is the process where a dedicated team physically finds, identifies and counts each item of stock in its location and records the item number and quantity. During this stage, as each item is individually counted, the inventory is established and overall inventory accuracy gradually increases roughly linearly.

The checking stage

The checking stage refers to the verification of the initial stock count before finalizing. It may include the following quality control procedures:

- the checking of any unreasonable counts where the count is deemed to be implausible
- the checking of stock known to be prone to error such as items with high risk or turnover
- the completion of variance reports, where a comparative inventory is available (such as a perpetual inventory or second stock count).

During the checking stage, stock count accuracy should theoretically further improve as item count errors are found and corrected.

The sampling stage

Generally, once the stock is counted and checked the resulting stock count inventory is assumed to be correct and used to generate stock valuations and update perpetual inventory records. However, if required a final sampling stage can be completed that tests the underlying stock count accuracy using statistical methods. This stage requires a representative and random sample of items to be chosen, recounted and compared to the stock count inventory. Item discrepancies greater than a pre-set tolerance are deemed to be errors, whereas those items that concur are considered accurate.

Importantly, the better the preparation, the steeper and higher the improvement in stock count accuracy as each item is counted during the stock count (see Figure 15.1). The better the counter and stock preparation, the faster and more accurate the stock count. During the checking stage there are more modest accuracy improvements (a gradual slope) as some count errors are found and corrected. During the sampling stage it is assumed that the inventory is not corrected further (hence a flat line), but sample stock is counted and compared to provide an estimate of the inventory's likely accuracy.

To be of benefit, the stock count's accuracy must surpass the accuracy of other already established inventories, each with its own level of accuracy. The dotted horizontal line in Figure 15.1 illustrates the accuracy of a perpetual inventory or previous stock count. The concept of four stock count stages illustrated here helps to more formally define the stock count process and accuracy over time.

15.2 A reference inventory

The accuracy of any stock count will be affected by the manner in which these four stages are executed. However, the extent to which procedural variations in these stages affect stock count accuracy is not well understood.

Presumably tidy, well-prepared stock is more easily counted than poorly-arranged stock, but can this effect be measured? Specifically, to what degree does speed and accuracy suffer if stock is well or poorly prepared?

Some counting procedures are likely to be better than others, but which are best and why? Likewise, some checking procedures will be better than others, but which provide the most accuracy in the least time?

Lastly, sample testing will provide an estimate of the underlying stock count accuracy, but how large a sample is needed?

Although a wide body of literature considers the inventory and its role in enterprise finance and stock control, there is little research that measures and answers such questions. Consequently, many books and articles that address operational procedures and best practice offer little scientific evidence to support their opinions. Even professional stock counters who can claim to have completed thousands of inventories have little hard data to support their methods.

The general lack of objective and rigorous analysis is largely due to the commercial realities of a busy enterprise. When comparing inventories it can be difficult to isolate the root cause of any discrepancy. It could lie in the perpetual inventory, in the stock count, or even in both. In a live, dynamic environment it is difficult to measure the accuracy or precision of a stock count when it is in fact being used to measure the accuracy of the perpetual inventory.

In order to systematically address questions about stock count accuracy, the stock must be fixed and an extremely accurate inventory of the stock established. With constant stock and an accurate reference inventory, stock counters can repeatedly count the stock in controlled conditions and their accuracy and duration compared to the known reference inventory. Under such conditions, variables like counter competency and the tidiness of the stock can be manipulated to determine their impact on stock count accuracy and duration.

15.3 A store with fixed stock

In 2008 an experimental stock count laboratory, modeled on a retail store, was established at the offices of RGIS LLC, an independent inventory service provider based in Auburn Hills, Michigan. The laboratory store consisted of everyday merchandise including dry grocery, variety items and clothing distributed across ordinary retail shelving. Figure 15.2 shows some of the gondolas, shelves and laboratory store stock that was either:

- tidy, where all like-items were neatly arranged in rows on each fixture and there was no mixing of items with different item numbers
- untidy, where similar-looking items which had different item numbers were blended together, much as if the store's merchandise had been moved around by customers.

Photographs were taken of each fixture with the same stock arranged under both conditions. These photographs were used to ensure that after each stock count the items could be returned to their required positions. Each of the 72 fixtures was labeled with a number for control, categorization and subsequent reporting.

Figure 15.2: Fixtures of experimental store stock.

Figure 15.3 shows the complete fixture floor plan of the laboratory store. The store contained 1400 unique item numbers (SKUs) with approximately 10,000 units (summarized in Figure 15.4). These were separated into 72 fixture locations throughout the store. Each fixture consisted of either shelves, display hooks or racking.

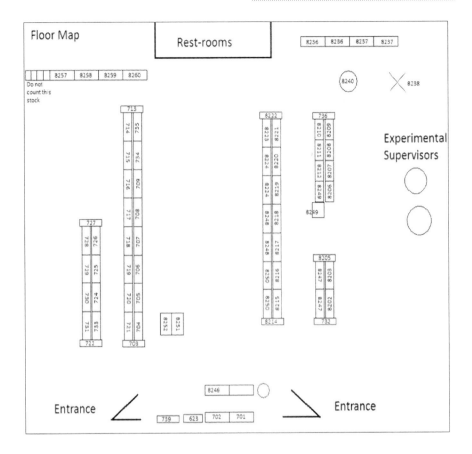

Figure 15.3: Floor plan of experimental store stock.

Unlike a normal trading enterprise, this store was never open for business. No stock was ever moved in or out, and the placement of the stock on the shelf was closely monitored to ensure that it was not appreciably rearranged or altered. And unlike a trading enterprise, the shop and its stock was in a fixed and secured area, only accessible by the experimenter and counters in a controlled way.

A reference inventory of the laboratory store stock was established after the stock was labeled and placed into the laboratory store. Using handheld computers a small, experienced and dedicated team was asked to barcode scan every item of stock, one at a time, inside the store. The total item quantities of each stock counter were then compared.

Any discrepancies were rigorously checked and corrected until there was a very high level of confidence that the reference inventory was a true and accurate representation of the laboratory store stock.

Once the reference inventory was established, other stock counters could count the stock under a range of experimental conditions, and by comparing their counts to the reference inventory their level of accuracy could be determined.

Fixtures	Unique items	Approx. units
72	1400	10,000

Figure 15.4: Number of fixtures, unique items and approximate total units in the laboratory store.

15.4 Summary

Four stock count stages

For convenience the stock count can be separated into four procedural stages: preparing, counting, checking and sampling.

A laboratory store with fixed stock

In order to measure inventory accuracy with a high level of confidence, a laboratory store was established with fixed stock levels and locations. Stock within the laboratory store was meticulously counted, recorded and verified several times in order to establish a reference inventory that described the items, quantities and locations. Once established, the laboratory stock and reference inventory was used as a benchmark to assess the performance of other stock counters under a range of stock and operational conditions.

16: Preparing stage

Having established a controlled laboratory store with a reference inventory, stock counter speed and accuracy could be measured under different conditions. In particular, the effect of variables such as stock counter competency and the level of stock preparation on inventory accuracy were assessed.

Both stock preparation and counter competence were expected to greatly influence the speed and accuracy of a stock count. In this chapter the magnitude of these effects is assessed.

16.1 Stock preparation: tidy and untidy

Well-marked and arranged stock is likely to be more easily and accurately counted than jumbled and poorly-arranged stock. During the course of the research, the laboratory store stock was either:

- tidy, where all like-items were neatly arranged in rows on each fixture and there was no mixing of items with different item numbers
- untidy, where similar-looking items which had different item numbers were blended together, much as if the store's merchandise had been moved around by customers.

Photographs were taken of each fixture with the same stock arranged under both conditions. These photographs were used to ensure that after each stock count the items could be returned to their required positions. Each of the 72 fixtures was labeled with a number for control, categorization and subsequent reporting. Figure 16.1 provides an example of a fixture with stock arranged in both a tidy and untidy manner.

Figure 16.1: Experimental store fixture showing the same stock well-prepared and tidy, and unprepared and untidy.

16.2 Counter competency levels

The stock counters were all volunteers and paid for their time. They were instructed to systematically, quickly and accurately enter each stock item number and count and record the item quantity.

All stock counters had previously been trained in basic stock count procedures and handheld device usage. At any time the counters could stop and ask questions of the laboratory store supervisor if anything was unclear.

Previous basic stock count training taught counters to:
- work systematically through each fixture; top to bottom, left to right
- identify and count each item separately
- work quickly and accurately.

Previous basic handheld device instructions taught counters how to:
- keypunch the fixture location number before commencing each fixture
- scan each item barcode, or where a barcode could not be scanned, keypunch the item number

- edit and correct an item number or quantity if an error occurred.

The counters were not given any quantity information and had to count and record each item themselves. This is sometimes called a 'blind count'.

The handheld device could be worn on the hip or held in the palm. Handheld devices consisted of a barcode reading laser, a data entry keyboard and a display screen (Figure 12.3 shows several different handheld devices).

In all, 81 individuals participated. As the laboratory store was quite small, no more than five counters completed their stock count at any one time.

Stock counters were categorized into three groups based on their previous stock count familiarity and competency:
- beginners with less than 50 hours' experience
- intermediates who typically had between 50 and 500 hours' experience
- experienced counters with more than 500 hours' experience.

Figure 16.2 shows the number of counters with each competency level who counted the stock under tidy and untidy conditions. Counters were allocated to the various conditions when available and as they volunteered. Unfortunately only five experienced counters were available during the untidy stock testing. However larger numbers of beginners and intermediates were available.

Total = 81	Beginner	Intermediate	Experienced
Tidy stock	10	10	10
Untidy stock	18	28	5

Figure 16.2: Number of counters in each of three competency levels.

16.3 Laboratory stock count data

Having established the laboratory store and reference inventory with two levels of stock preparation (tidy and untidy) and three levels of competence (experienced, intermediate and beginner) the stock was counted.

The following information was recorded for each data entry:
- shelf and fixture number
- item number (SKU)
- quantity
- data entry method (barcode scanning or keypunching)
- quantity entry method (single quantities or quantity greater than one)
- time (for each data entry from start to finish)
- item error (where each item count was compared to the reference count).

The resulting stock count data-set consisted of around 200,000 individual scanned or keypunched item record entries. Since some item numbers were scanned more than once by a counter, this data was collapsed to over 100,000 unique records consisting of counter, item number and quantity.

16.4 Tidy and untidy stock

Recall that each count error was defined as any difference exceeding a specified tolerance between an item quantity and its corresponding reference quantity. In the analysis, a tolerance of 0% was typically used where any discrepancy between the reference item quantity and the stock count item quantity was defined as an error. The total number of errors for each counter was expressed as a percentage relative to the total number of items present in the store environment.

Figure 16.3 presents the average error differences between stock counters in the two environments—tidy and untidy.

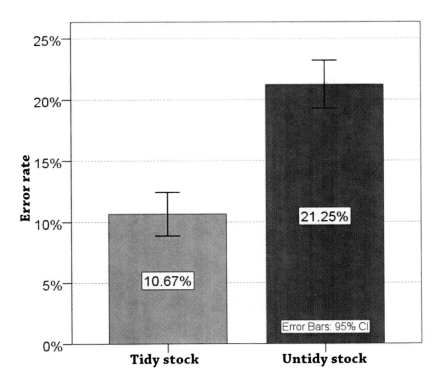

Figure 16.3: Average stock count error rates when the stock was tidy and untidy.

The average error rate (with zero tolerance) for tidy stock was 10%, whereas it was 21% for untidy stock. (Allowing up to ±5% tolerance on all counts 'decreased' the error rate by around 30%.) The error bars on each graph indicate the 95% confidence interval (that the true underlying error will be found within this range 95% of the time).

Note that even though the physical stock was identical (same location, item and quantities) the error rate doubled when the stock was untidy and poorly prepared. This suggests that ensuring stock is tidy, marked, and arranged with correct facings before a stock count can halve the likely number of stock count errors.

Figure 16.4 shows the average deviation percentage calculated for both tidy and untidy stock. Once again the deviation was almost half that observed in poor preparation condition.

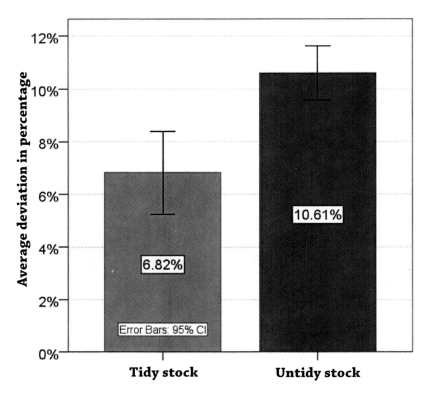

Figure 16.4: Average quantity deviation percentage when the stock was tidy and untidy.

Figure 16.5 shows the average duration of counts when the stock was tidy and untidy. Note that, on average, to count the untidy stock required 163 minutes, whereas the tidy stock took 136 minutes. That is, it took 27 minutes or 16% less time to count the same stock when it was tidy than when it was untidy.

16.5 Counter competency and error

Figure 16.6 shows the error rate for the three experience levels counting tidy and untidy stock. Essentially, when counting tidy stock, experienced counters made significantly fewer errors (8%) than inexperienced counters (13.9%) (where the 95% confidence interval for experienced error rate lay outside the mean of the beginners' error rate).

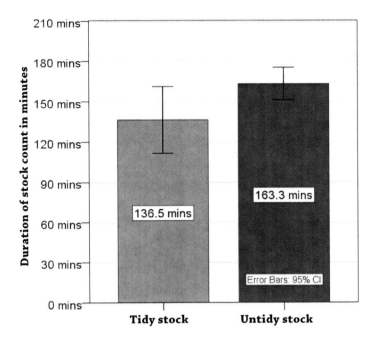

Figure 16.5: Average stock count duration when the stock was tidy and untidy.

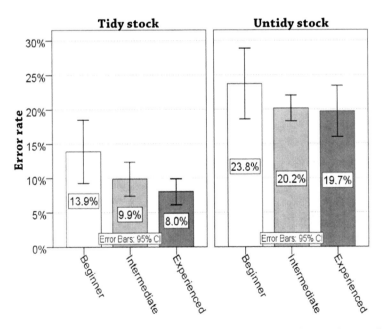

Figure 16.6: Stock count error rates with tidy and untidy stock for counters with different competency levels.

However, there was much greater error variability and no significant difference between the three groups when counting untidy stock. While experienced counters were more accurate than beginners when counting tidy stock, they were little better if the stock was poorly prepared and untidy.

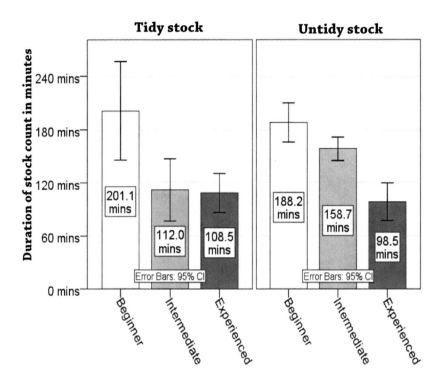

Figure 16.7: Stock count duration rates using tidy and untidy stock for counters with different competency levels.

Figure 16.7 considers the speed of the counters when counting tidy and untidy stock. The duration of the stock count was calculated as the time taken to count each item summed for all items counted. The duration measured only included the actual counting of stock and excluded briefing time, rest breaks, and the processing of the handheld data.

The 10 beginner tidy stock counters took an average of 8.6 seconds to count each item (201.1 min/1400 items) whereas the 18 beginner untidy stock counters took 8.1 seconds per item (188.2 min/1400 items). This difference was negligible and insignificant. Presumably beginners used few time-saving count strategies and their stock count duration did not improve with tidy stock.

The 10 intermediate tidy stock counters were significantly faster (112 minutes) than the 28 untidy stock counters (158.7 minutes). Intermediate counters were almost as fast as experienced counters of tidy stock, but lost this advantage when counting untidy stock.

Lastly, the 10 experienced tidy stock counters were slower (108.5 minutes) than the 5 untidy stock counters (98.5 minutes); however, the sample size was small and the difference was not significant. It appeared that when the stock was tidy, experienced counters were fast and accurate, but when the stock was untidy—while they were just as fast—their error rate more than doubled (see Figure 16.6).

Experienced counters were certainly more familiar with the handheld equipment. Unlike beginners they rarely had to look at the keyboard or screen as they entered data. They also reported using counting strategies such as counting in pairs, rows and dozens. It seemed likely that using these strategies made them fast, but they relied on the stock being neat. Using the strategies when the stock was untidy maintained speed, but added error.

16.6 Counter speed versus accuracy

Figure 16.8 presents each counter's stock count error rate plotted against their stock count duration. The data largely clustered in the center indicates almost no correlation or relationship between an individual's speed or accuracy when counting tidy or untidy stock ($r = 0.03$ and $r = 0.093$ respectively). In practice this makes choosing stock counters difficult. Knowing a stock counter is fast or slow does not predict whether they will be accurate or inaccurate. Certainly, if counters choose to count more slowly, they can probably improve their accuracy (see Figure 16.8); however, there is no fixed relationship between speed and accuracy across counters. Each counter's speed and accuracy are independent and one does not determine the other.

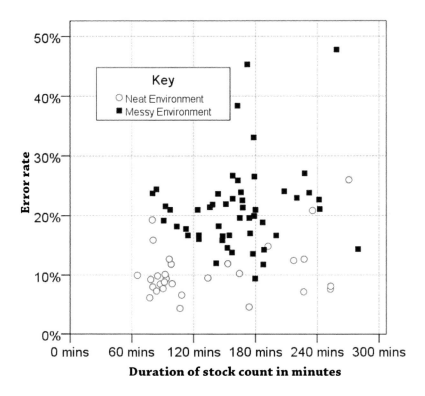

Figure 16.8: Number of errors compared to stock count duration for counters of tidy and untidy stock.

16.7 Summary

A laboratory store

A laboratory store with fixed stock and a reference inventory was established to examine the accuracy and duration of various stages in the stock count process. Using handheld computers, a range of grocery, clothing and variety stock items were counted. Eighty-one counters were asked to count the same stock in a range of conditions.

Preparing stage

Two aspects of stock count preparation were examined: tidy and untidy stock and the level of stock counter competency (beginner, intermediate and experienced).

Error and duration rates

Generally, counting stage error rates in tidy stock reached about 10% and in untidy areas error was about 20%. On average, the counting duration for tidy stock was around 16% less than untidy stock (163 minutes versus 137 minutes).

Counting or identifying

People counted accurately regardless of their stock counting competency. This is perhaps not surprising as we are taught to count at an early age and practice it throughout our lives.

Although people could count, they had difficulty identifying stock, especially when it was poorly organized. Stock count practice and familiarity improved identification competency, but only when the stock was tidy and neatly arranged.

There was no relationship between individual stock counters' speed and accuracy. Being accurate did not predict speed or vice-versa.

17: Counting stage

When completing a stock count, counters make occasional errors. Certainly these can be reduced if the stock is well prepared, but they cannot necessarily be eliminated entirely. In this chapter the types of counting errors are examined, given the nature of the stock and selected stock count procedures.

The counting stage is often called a 'blind count' because the stock counter is generally not (and should not be) informed of the expected item quantity. People only count and record the items that they systematically find during their stock count. The ability to reliably and accurately identify and count stock is central to all stock count practice.

17.1 Types of error

In the laboratory store, an error was defined as any item's quantity difference between the reference inventory and a stock counter's inventory. However any differences did not indicate the cause or type of error. In order to understand why, on average, experienced counters commit fewer errors than beginners, it was necessary to consider and isolate the types of errors made.

One frequent error type was to miss an item number (SKU) altogether. This sometimes happened when an item was hidden from view, perhaps at the rear of a shelf, when it was mixed with other like-items or even when counters missed an entire shelf or area altogether. Any item number that was in the reference inventory but not counted in the stock count inventory was categorized as being missed. On average, 3.5% of unique item numbers were missed for tidy stock and 8.4% for untidy stock.

A second error type occurred when a counter simply miscounted the quantity of an item. They identified the item properly, but their count was incorrect. In order to gauge the counter's ability to count the right quantity, regardless of the item number, the total number of units for each counter and location were compared to the total number for each location in the reference inventory. The average location had a quantity of 129 items with a range of 12 to 761 and a standard deviation of 118.

Figures 17.1 and 17.2 provide frequency distributions showing the location quantity deviation as a percentage for tidy and untidy stock. The vertical lines highlight a difference of ±5%; that is, where a counter in a location counted ±5% of the total stock quantity observed in that location in the reference inventory. Note the number of count deviations is higher in the untidy stock distribution because there were more counters tested in that condition.

Most counters were clearly within 5% of the reference inventory quantity for each location. This suggested that within a location the correct number of stock units was counted. However, they were often allocated to the wrong items numbers.

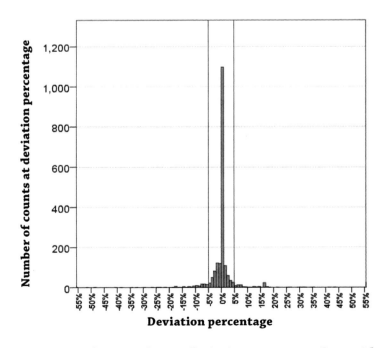

Figure 17.1: Distribution of count deviation percentage for untidy stock.

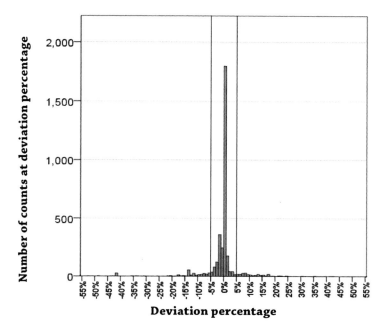

Figure 17.2: Distribution of count deviation percentage for tidy stock.

Figure 17.3: Nine cans of dog food with five unique item numbers (SKUs) marked A to E.

A third type of error was item misallocation. When faced with a selection of similar-looking items, counters incorrectly included the unique item with another similar but different item number.

Figure 17.3 shows nine cans of dog food arranged exactly as they were in the untidy stock environment. The characters A to E superimposed on each item indicate a unique item number.

Figure 17.4 shows the distribution of quantities allocated to each of these item numbers (A to E) for all counters. Note that 96% of counters agreed that there were nine cans in total and only 4% counted either one too many or one too few. However, counters were not consistently able to allocate the correct quantities to the correct item type. For example, only 34% of counters correctly identified that there was one can of item number C and 64% of counters missed item B altogether. This highlights a common occurrence: when stock is disorganized and very similar in appearance, it is easily misidentified and allocated to the wrong item number.

Unfortunately these three error types (missed, miscounted and misallocated) could not be absolutely separated. For example, in some cases an item thought to be missed may have actually been misallocated. Nevertheless, by defining these error types and by measuring their proportional magnitude, their relevance could be better understood.

The three categories were defined such that:

- item numbers that were not counted at all represented missed items
- items that had quantity discrepancies of equal or less than 5% were defined as miscounted quantity errors
- items that had quantity discrepancies greater than ±5% represented misallocated items.

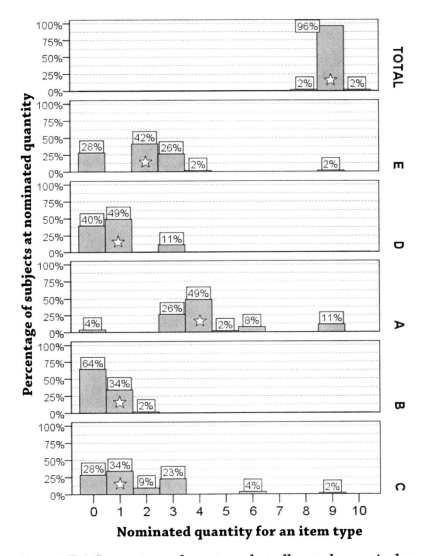

Figure 17.4: Percentage of counters that allocated a particular quantity to each item. The star represents the true quantity.

A quantity discrepancy of 5% was used to distinguish between miscounted and misallocated error. This value was chosen because the distribution of error deviations for each location suggested the magnitude of quantity error was small—generally 5% or less (see Figures 17.1 and 17.2).

Figures 17.5 and 17.6 provide bar-graphs of the total and individual error types for the three counter competency levels for both tidy and untidy stock. Note that the sum of the three error types equals the total error (the panel on the far right).

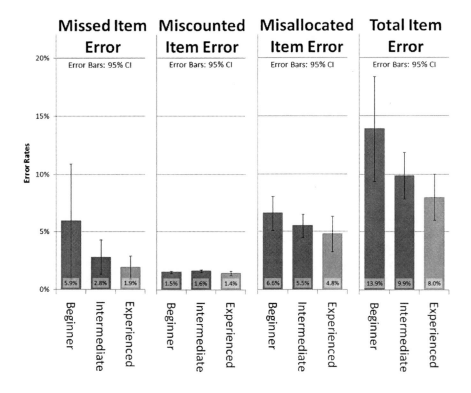

Figure 17.5: Item error rates for tidy stock separated into missed, miscounted, misallocated and total error.

The proportion of miscount error was reasonably small and constant regardless of competency level or stock condition. However, the proportion of missed and misallocated error was significantly higher for beginners than intermediates and experienced counters. This suggested that experienced counters were better at identifying stock, but were little better at counting it.

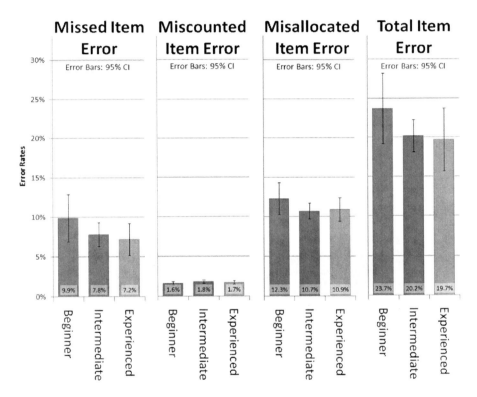

Figure 17.6: Item error rates for untidy stock separated into missed, miscounted, misallocated and total error.

17.2 Error distributions for each item

The characteristics of each item in the experimental store differ significantly (in quantity, appearance, location and so on). These factors influenced the ease with which each item could be accurately counted. By analyzing the distribution of counts for individual items, it was possible to gain insights into the counting strategies used by individuals.

Consider a common occurrence for items with a large quantity (greater than 100). Figure 17.7 shows two small boxes of drink sachets as they appeared in the laboratory store. Each box (front and back) was compartmentalized into three sections, each containing three rows of about 30 units.

Figure 17.8 shows a frequency histogram illustrating the number of counters and their count for this item. The fine vertical line represents the true quantity of 189 units that was recorded in the reference inventory.

Figure 17.7: Boxes with six rows of drink sachets.

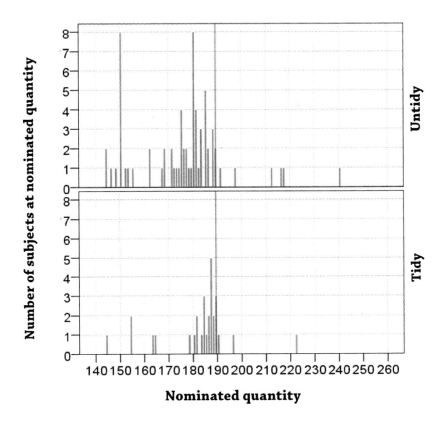

Figure 17.8: Distribution of drink sachet quantities for all counters.
True quantity was 189 units.

Only five counters obtained the correct quantity of 189 units. On
average, these counters took just under four minutes (232 seconds) to
count the item, whereas those with errors took just over two minutes
(133 seconds).

This indicated that those who spent more time counting large
quantity items were rewarded with greater accuracy. Other counters
appeared to merely count one row and applied this sample to all of
the rows. This is shown in Figure 17.8 using untidy stock. The error
distribution is bi-modal with two distinct peaks: at 150 corresponding to six rows with 25 items, and the other at 180 corresponding
to six rows with 30 items. This was further supported anecdotally.

Experienced counters verbally reported that in order to save time they would count in multiples.

Perhaps this behavior reflects human nature. The stock counters wanted to complete the task quickly and if the stock was perceived to be of little value (and thus small deviations in the reported quantities were unlikely to have an effect on the enterprise), people chose to approximate the count rather than counting each item individually. They effectively applied their own commercial tolerances, whether prompted to or not.

17.3 Stock department and error

The counting of clothes, tinned groceries or cosmetics (make-up) are very different tasks. Clothes are typically hung from a rack or folded in stacks, groceries are stacked in rows, and cosmetics may be hung from peg-board wall systems. Not surprisingly, different types of stock, stored in different ways, generated different rates of stock count error.

The stock in the laboratory store was divided into 21 departments based on its physical characteristics. The average department had 63 item numbers. The stock count error rate and types of error for each stock department in tidy and untidy conditions is presented in Figures 17.9 and 17.10.

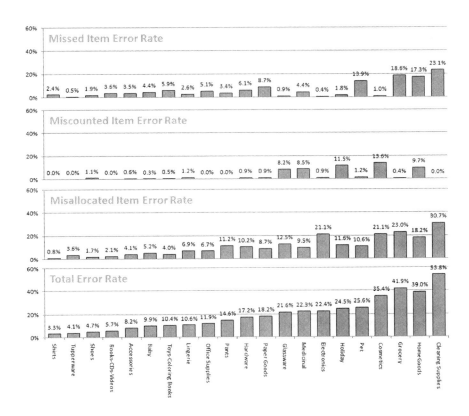

Figure 17.9: Department error rates for untidy stock in order of magnitude.

Consider two departments with similar overall error rates in untidy conditions: cosmetics and grocery. Cosmetics were characterized by large quantities and complicated peg-board shelving. Even when neatly organized it was difficult to count accurately. Consequently stock counters made many miscounting and misallocation errors in both untidy (12.5% and 21.6%) and tidy (13.6% and 21.1%) conditions.

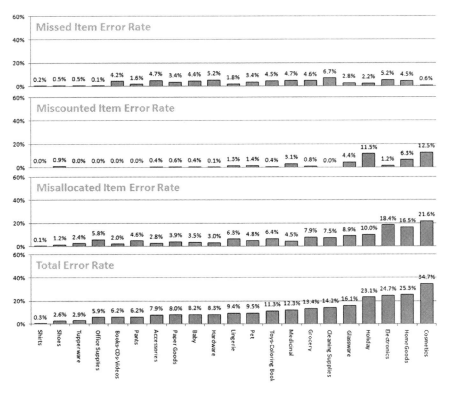

Figure 17.10: Department error rates for tidy stock in order of magnitude.

Stock in the grocery department was characterized on the other hand by smaller quantities and large numbers of mixed but unique items on shelves. Consequently, very little miscounting error was observed (0.4%) when the stock was untidy, but large numbers of misallocation and missed items error occurred due to identification issues (23.0% and 18.6% respectively). This was evidenced by the sharp decline of these errors when counting tidy stock (7.9% and 4.6%).

These results again confirm that identification errors were common for items such as grocery varieties that looked similar, but were poorly organized on the shelf.

17.4 Automatic and keyed scanning

Handheld computers use software and are programmable. As such, their features (display and data entry method) can be optimized to facilitate the stock count process. Using a handheld device, a counter normally scans or keypunches an item number and then keypunches the stock quantity. The stock quantity may be any number of one or more. This facility is called 'keyed quantity number' or KQn.

Another feature of the handheld device is single quantity scanning, allowing the counter to merely scan one item barcode and then scan the next item. The handheld device automatically allocates a count of 1 to the first scanned item entered. This facility, automatic quantity of 1 or AQ1, accelerates data entry for single unit items.

In the laboratory, store counters were allowed to use the AQ1 facility as they wished. During training it was recommended for adjacent items that were difficult to distinguish. Accordingly, books, movies, music, vintage wines and racked clothing all lend themselves to AQ1 item entry. The reason is that stock such as clothes can look very similar, be of the same brand, color and style, but nonetheless have different item numbers due to a different size, or some other indistinct feature. For the purpose of collecting an inventory, however, it is important to determine the exact quantities of all sizes individually, whether for replenishment or sales optimization purposes.

Scanning results overall

The different speed and accuracy rates for KQn and AQ1 stock quantities were analyzed. Figure 17.11 presents the results for untidy stock.

All of the different items in the laboratory store were categorized according to their number of units. There were 5 categories: items with a quantity of 1, items with a quantity of 2 to 4 and so on, up to items with a quantity greater than 30.

The KQn and AQ1 error rates and the time to count each unit of quantity in seconds were compared across the 5 quantity categories.

Qty category	KQn Error rate %	KQn Time rate secs/unit	AQ1 Error rate %	AQ1 Time rate secs/unit
1	11.7	3.28	1.0	2.89
2–4	19.2	1.94	6.3	3.31
5–9	23.6	1.51	17.8	3.33
10–29	25.0	0.97	22.1	2.89
30+	37.2	0.91	44.1	2.48

Figure 17.11: Comparison of scanning rates counting untidy stock.

For quantities less than 5, AQ1 was a superior method of scanning stock. Its error rate was 3 to 10 times lower than KQn. Its duration was much the same for a quantity of 1 and about 30% slower for quantities up to 5.

For quantities greater than 5, the ideal method was more complex. AQ1 speed remained constant at around 3 seconds per unit, whereas KQn speed decreased steadily until it was less than 1 second per unit. At this time the error rates of both methods became comparable, as misallocation error—common to small quantities—decreased, and miscounting error increased. Miscounting error tended to affect KQn scanning and AQ1 scanning to similar extents, but for possibly different reasons.

The KQn and AQ1 time rates were comparable for difficult stock, but the accuracy rate of AQ1 scanning was generally superior. The results suggest that if stock was poorly prepared and subjectively difficult to count it should be AQ1 scanned, even if the number of units was large.

Scanning results for competency levels

KQn and AQ1 error rates were also examined with regard to counter competency levels. It was plausible that the additional cognitive load of having to operate a numeric key pad might contribute to the error rate for a beginner stock counter, and that this additional level of complexity should only be introduced once a sufficient level of competency had been obtained.

Experienced				
Qty category	KQn error rate %	KQn time rate secs/unit	AQ1 error rate %	AQ1 time rate secs/unit
1	12.9	1.7	0.7	2.2
2–4	19.4	0.9	4.1	2.5
5–9	17.8	0.7	15.2	2.6
10–29	24.1	0.5	20.0	1.9
30+	36.5	0.4	***†	***†
Intermediates				
Qty category	KQn error rate %	KQn time rate secs/unit	AQ1 error rate %	AQ1 time rate secs/unit
1	12.9	3.2	0.9	3.2
2–4	18.2	1.7	6.25	3.5
5–9	18.35	1.2	18.3	3.6
10–29	23.9	0.9	26.8	2.9
30+	38.7	0.7	53.5	2.6
Beginners				
Qty category	KQn error rate %	KQn time rate secs/unit	AQ1 error rate %	AQ1 time rate secs/unit
1	12.4	3.6	1.8	3.2
2–4	19.6	2.1	6.9	3.5
5–9	19.1	1.5	18.2	3.6
10–29	24.8	1.1	13.0	2.9
30+	39.3	0.9	35.75	2.6

† Note that no stock with a quantity of 30 or more was ever counted using the AQ1 method. Consequently the error rate and time rate in this condition.

Figure 17.12: Comparison of scanning rates for experienced, intermediate and beginner counters.

This line of reasoning, however, was not supported by the data. Figure 17.12 indicates that there were no observed differences between counter competency levels. This suggested that the effective use of

AQ1 techniques benefits all counters, not just beginners. To maximize accuracy and speed, AQ1 techniques should be used selectively for stock with low units and high identification difficulty. Stacked clothing in different sizes would be a prime example.

17.5 Summary

Three defined types of stock count error

Stock count errors in the laboratory store were arranged into three types: missed item numbers (not counted at all); miscounted items (with a quantity discrepancy of less than or equal to 5%) and misallocated items (with a quantity discrepancy greater than 5%).

Few unit counting errors

The miscounting of an item's quantity was the least frequent type of error and did not vary greatly when counting tidy or untidy stock. Counters could count the number of units in any location rather accurately.

Identification errors are frequent

Missed items and misallocated items roughly doubled when the stock was untidy. Counters might often count the correct quantity, but allocated this across the wrong item numbers.

Untidy stock undermines the value of experience

If the stock was untidy, experienced counters were only slightly more accurate than beginners. Stock count familiarity added little if the stock was difficult to separate and identify.

Using counting strategies

Counters reported that they often counted in multiples (tens, dozens, etc.) but this led to large errors if the wrong multiple was used.

Stock department and error

Error rates varied widely across stock departments, depending on the nature and the manner of stock presentation. Not surprisingly, similar-looking stock, closely arranged, was more prone to counting error.

AQ1 is better than KQn for quantities less than 5

For quantities of 5 or less, item units counted individually (AQ1) took little extra time and resulted in 3 to 10 times less error than items with units counted together (KQn). Scanning each unit individually was far more accurate than identifying item numbers and counting the total units.

18: Checking stage

During the preparing stage, in order to facilitate a fast and accurate stock count, stock counters are chosen and briefed, equipment readied, and stock marked, tidied and arranged. The counting stage follows where the initial stock count of all items is completed. Ideally, using handheld devices or stock sheets, counters work systematically through each location and record each stock item number and quantity.

The accuracy and duration of the entire stock count is not determined by the count stage alone. Often a number of unit and item checks are completed either during or immediately after counting to ensure that all stock was identified and correctly counted. Some checks are simple and commonsense manual processes, while others are automated and integrated into the computer systems. However, their benefit, duration and cost are often not understood or formally measured.

Any useful stock count check procedure must improve inventory accuracy by identifying and correcting a large number of item and quantity errors in a commercially viable amount of time.

This chapter considers the nature of location checks and item checks and tests their effectiveness in the laboratory store.

18.1 Location checking

Even the largest and most complex stock count can be simplified by separating areas of stock into discrete and numbered locations. Each location effectively becomes a smaller and simpler stock count in its own right. Checking that all locations are completed is a simple way to isolate issues and ensure all stock is counted.

There are two common forms of location checks: location completion checks and location unit checks. Each is discussed below.

Location completion checks

A location completion check is the act of simply ensuring that all locations have been counted during a stock count. Each stock area can be marked with a numbered location ticket. These numbers are also recorded on a location list or applied to a visual fixture floor plan.

As locations are allocated and counted, a stock count supervisor marks the location on the list or floor plan. Also, before beginning a location, the counter keypunches the location number into a designated field on the handheld device. When the handheld data is subsequently transferred to a computer it can be processed and a location summary list generated.

By recording and checking that all locations are counted, any duplicated or missed areas of stock are more easily identified and rectified. Since any missed items are by definition in error, correcting them will only improve overall inventory accuracy.

The number of items or units allocated to a location is arbitrary. Generally, locations are defined according to the physical attributes of the stock racking and placement. In retail settings a location with about 100 units is common.

Figure 18.1: Fixture with area ticket.

In a clothing or book store this roughly corresponds to each shelf, whereas in a grocery store it might be a gondola bay or fixture. In warehousing and distribution environments, since stock is already allocated to numbered bins, a location ticket is redundant. Figure 18.1 shows a retail fixture with a location ticket attached to its top left corner.

Location unit checks

Another location checking procedure is to count the number of units in a location and compare this to the counter's total units. This is sometimes called a location unit check.

Typically, a counter using a handheld device counts and records all items and units. On completing the fixture, the handheld device automatically calculates and displays the total number of units in the fixture (i.e. the sum of all item quantities). The counter writes this total as well as their name or initials on the location ticket. This indicates the fixture's completion.

A location unit check is completed when a second independent person counts all units in the fixture, ignoring specific item numbers. Their location count total is compared to the stock counter's unit count recorded on the location ticket. If the two differ by more than an acceptable tolerance (say 3%), the location is deemed likely to contain a high number of errors and requires each item to be recounted.

Location completion and unit checks both help to identify duplicated or missed locations. A location completion check also tests the likely integrity of the stock counter's total unit count for a location. However, the location unit check has some limitations:

- Other types of stock count checks (using reasonability and variance reports discussed below) only check items with a high probability of error. By contrast, during a location unit check all items in a location are counted, independently of the stock count. This process will add more time to the stock count duration.
- If a location unit check identifies a location that requires recounting, all of its items are then recounted. This is likely to include

both correctly and incorrectly counted items. In practice the likelihood of a location unit check improving the accuracy of the stock count is merely the chance that one stock counter works more accurately than another. The effectiveness of a location unit check therefore lies solely in its ability to locate highly error-prone locations and replace these areas with at least an average stock counter's accuracy.

- A location unit check can only identify missed or miscounted quantities. It cannot highlight items that were only misallocated. Findings in the laboratory store suggested that about half of all errors are misallocations (see Figure 17.6). Therefore its effectiveness is restricted.

Despite these limitations, location completeness checks are popular among some enterprise managers and frequently used to check stock count accuracy. It is assumed that location checks are fast and convenient. In the laboratory store the duration of location checks was analyzed.

Location unit check duration

The laboratory store consisted of 72 display fixtures with stock. Each fixture was called a location and marked with a numbered ticket. A location check list was generated. This listed all of the location numbers and the total location quantity randomly drawn from earlier stock counts (see Chapter 17).

Twelve paid counters were then asked to count the total number of units (items x quantity) observed in each location and record these onto the location check list.

The location count quantities were compared with the stock count quantities. If there was a unit difference the items and quantities recorded in the stock count were discarded, and all items in the location were counted again.

The average time taken to complete the location unit checks was compared to the average time required to stock count the same stock. Figure 18.2 presents the results. It took 192 minutes to count the

1400 tidy stock items, whereas it took 228 minutes to count the same stock when untidy. The average location check times were similar with 197 minutes for tidy stock and 205 minutes for untidy stock.

	Tidy duration	Untidy duration
Average stock count total	192	228
Average location check total	197	205

Figure 18.2: Total duration in minutes to stock count and location-check all items.

Basically it took as much time to complete a location unit check as it did to count each item. It seemed that the time taken to data-enter each item with a handheld device added little to stock count duration compared to the time moving between locations and actually physically counting the stock.

In general, location completion checking is likely to improve stock count accuracy. It helps to control the flow of the stock count and identify all error types (missed, misallocated and miscounted). Location unit checking, where the total units in a location are counted, can take almost as much time as counting the stock item by item. As it only detects missed or miscounted stock, it appears of limited value.

18.2   Item checking

While location checking considers all units within a location, item checking considers specific items that are thought likely to be in error. Two common forms of item checking are reasonability and variance checks. These rely on management experience, numeric algorithms or comparative inventories to identify items with a high probability of stock count error that require recounting.

Reasonability checking

Once a stock count is completed and an inventory generated it can be printed and reviewed. Often the same items cause problems at every stock count. Competent enterprise managers, glancing at the inventory of items and units, will identify items that look unlikely to be correct and warrant checking. That is, the item stock count units look 'unreasonable'.

These may be item varieties that are known to be difficult to identify or count, have large trading volumes, high value or are risky and prone to theft or damage. Item quantities that appear improbably high or low are easily recognized and can indicate either identification or counting errors.

Some perpetual and stock count computer systems include algorithms that arithmetically identify items that are likely to be in error. Examples include:

- items observed in the perpetual inventory with positive quantities not observed in the stock count (i.e. missed items)
- items within a location with a stock quantity more than twice the average of that location
- items with quantities that exceed normal weekly stock holdings for that item line by a factor of two or more.

There are two important limiting factors on the efficacy of reasonability checks:

- the experience and knowledge of the enterprise manager in choosing the appropriate criteria for 'unreasonable' stock quantities
- the ability of these automated procedures to efficiently find errors. For example, algorithms that depend on large average quantity multiples for a location may produce many false alarms in areas with non-uniform quantities across items.

Variance checks

Variance checking is where a stock count inventory is compared to another inventory source in order to identify items likely to be incorrectly counted.

Generally, each item in the stock count is matched with its corresponding item from a perpetual inventory or secondary stock count and any quantity discrepancies reported. Any large discrepancies between items suggest possible counting errors. Variance reports are usually printed in variance quantity magnitude or item value order, highlighting the largest discrepancies that are most in need of checking.

The variance report is basically using one inventory to verify the accuracy of another. Any discrepancies are thought to be errors. The weakness of this approach is that the comparative inventory must be highly accurate if it is to identify errors in the stock count, rather than wasting time identifying items that are in fact correct.

18.3 Evaluating checking procedures

When evaluating the effectiveness of a checking procedure, one must consider:

- Its accuracy consists of the rate at which genuine errors are corrected and correct items are made incorrect. If the former is not high enough, or the latter is too high, then the check procedure is not only a waste of time but can potentially increase overall stock count error.
- The ratio between the number of errors the check procedure identifies and the number of items checked. If the check procedure finds a high proportion of errors relative to checked items, it is likely to increase accuracy.
- The time taken to generate and complete the checking procedure adds to the duration of the total stock count. If the check procedure takes little time to find and correct, it will be cost-effective. However, if it finds few errors and takes a long period of time, it will be of little benefit.

Ideally the check procedure should only suggest items that are in error. Unfortunately, in reality some items designated for checking will include items that are not in error. Similarly, when counters return to the physical stock and check items, their recounts will be correct only part of the time. The check procedure is only valuable if its accuracy rate is greater than the initial stock count's over the same items or locations. Figure 18.3 summarizes the performance of any stock count check procedure. The different possible final item quantities are expressed as proportions 'a', 'b', 'c' and 'd'.

A useful reasonability or variance check report will identify items with incorrect stock quantities (i.e. errors). If all items on the report are errors, and all items are corrected, all items would fall in cell 'c'.

Status of items		Check counter	
		Correct	Incorrect
Check report	Correct	a	b
	Incorrect	c	d

Figure 18.3: Correct and incorrect stock counts on a check report, compared to correct and incorrect re-counts by a check counter.

In practice, not all items on the check report are actually checked correctly. After checking, some items remain in error and are represented in cell 'd'. The sum of cells 'c' and 'd' reflects all items which were true errors on the report.

Unfortunately the check report itself is also imperfect and will include some items that are already correct and do not need checking. Those items that remain correct after checking are in cell 'a', and those that are made incorrect even though they were correct in the initial stock count are in cell 'b'.

In order to know how good a check procedure is, one must measure the proportion of items in cells 'b' and 'c'. The ideal check procedure would have 'b' as close to 0% and 'c' as close to 100% as possible. Items in cells 'a' and 'd' do not change overall accuracy since they are correct or incorrect in the check report and remain so after checking.

Mathematically the merit of a check procedure can be calculated using the following formula:

$$\text{Final accuracy} = \text{Initial accuracy} + \frac{N_c}{N}(c-b)$$

Where:
- N_c is the number of items involved with the check procedure or its scope
- N is the total number of items in the environment
- c is the percentage of inaccurate items on the completed check report which were accurately checked by the stock counter
- b is the percentage of accurate items on the completed check report which were inaccurately checked by the stock counter.

The ratio of $\frac{N_c}{N}$ reflects the number of items checked compared to the total number of stock count items. If the number of checks is small (N_c) relative to the total number of stock count items (N), its value will always be limited.

In the laboratory store, reasonability and variance check procedures were tested experimentally. The time and the number of errors found and corrected were collected and analyzed. The duration of location check procedures was also evaluated.

Reasonability checks

Recall that a laboratory store with about 1400 items and a total of about 10,000 units was established at the RGIS facilities in Auburn Hills, Michigan. This shop never traded and all of the stock fixtures, items and units were known and recorded in a reference inventory.

Previously a group of 51 people counted the stock when it was tidy and another group of 30 counted the same stock when it was untidily arranged on the fixtures and shelves. This resulted in 81 inventories of the same stock for comparison and analysis.

The 51 stock counts with untidy stock were used to generate items that were reasonably likely to have counting errors. For each counter, items with a quantity greater than twice the average item quantity (a multiple of two) within a location were deemed sufficiently likely to be counting errors. Four hundred items with the largest multiples across all counters were randomly allocated to four unique reasonability check reports, giving 100 items in each report.

Sixteen counters were then randomly allocated to one of the four reasonability reports. The counters were paid for their time, about four hours, and asked to work as quickly and as accurately as they could. Each systematically matched each item on the reasonability report with the physical stock on the shelf. They recounted the physical stock and recorded its quantity and any discrepancy on the reasonability report. Eight counters conducted their checks when the stock was tidy and eight counters completed their checks when the stock was untidy.

The results were averaged across the four lists giving over 1500 data points (not all counters completely finished their 100 items on their reports). The findings are shown as percentages in Figure 18.4.

$(N_c = 100, N = 1400)$		**Check counter**		
		Correct	**Incorrect**	**Totals**
Check report	**Correct**	38.5%	6.5%	45.0%
	Incorrect	35.4%	19.6%	55.0%
	Totals	73.9%	26.1%	100%

Figure 18.4: Tidy stock reasonability check procedure.

Note that 55% of check report items had counting errors. Accordingly, the remaining 45% of items that required checking were not in error. Independent of this, the average check counter achieved 73.9% accuracy.

Interestingly, 38.5% of items were not in error and after checking remained not in error. Similarly, 19.6% were in error and after checking remained in error. Clearly the status of these items was not changed when checked and so overall inventory accuracy was not changed. The 35.4% of items that were in error, then checked and corrected, improved overall accuracy, but this was reduced by the 6.5% of items that were correct initially but which were made incorrect after checking.

In summary, the reasonability check procedure for tidy stock improved the accuracy of the inventory by 2.1% (since $N_c = 100$, $N = 1400$, $b = 6.5$, and $c = 35.4$, where $100 / 1400 \times (35.4\% - 6.5\%) = 2.1\%$).

Figure 18.5 presents the same procedure using untidy stock. The reasonability report was more valuable for untidy stock because it identified more true errors for correction (79.8% for untidy stock in Figure 18.5 compared to 55% for tidy stock in Figure 18.4).

This suggested that untidy items with high units (greater than twice the average) were more likely to be genuine counting errors. Overall, the reasonability check procedure improved the inventory accuracy by 3.9% (since $N_c = 100$, $N = 1400$, $b = 59.3$ and $c = 4$, where $100 / 1400 \times (59.3\% - 4.0\%) = 3.9\%$).

Reasonability checks with untidy stock were more useful than those using tidy stock, although the final accuracy obtained was still lower.

(N_c = 100, N = 1400)		Check counter		
		Correct	Incorrect	Totals
Check report	Correct	16.2%	4.0%	20.2%
	Incorrect	59.3%	20.5%	79.8%
	Totals	75.5%	24.5%	100%

Figure 18.5: Untidy stock reasonability check procedure.

Variance checks

In order to generate variance checks, the data for 10 tidy stock counts and 10 untidy stock counts were randomly selected. Each group was arranged in pairs and used to represent the first and second stock count inventories for comparison.

Five variance reports for tidy stock and five for untidy stock were generated. These listed all of the item quantity discrepancies in magnitude order. The largest 100 discrepancies were printed and used for checking. These were approximately distributed over two-thirds of the 72 stock locations.

Seven counters were randomly allocated to check the tidy stock variance reports in tidy stock conditions, and eight used untidy stock variance reports in untidy stock conditions. The counters were paid for their time, about four hours, and asked to work as quickly and as accurately as they could.

Each thoroughly matched items on the variance report with the physical stock on the shelf. They recounted the physical stock and recorded its quantity and any discrepancy on the variance report. The results were combined giving just under 1500 data points (a few counters did completely finish).

Figures 18.6 and 18.7 present the findings for the variance checks using tidy and untidy stock. Note that for tidy stock, less than half of the items identified on the variance report were actually incorrect in the first place (43.7%). Also, the total accuracy improvement was only 20.7% and this was offset by the addition of 17% error.

Overall the variance report for tidy stock improved accuracy by a negligible 0.3% on average (since $N_C = 100$, $N = 1400$, $b = 17.0$ and $c = 20.7$, where $100 / 1400 \times 20.7\% - 17\% = 0.3\%$). This suggested that given tidy stock with high levels of counting accuracy, the checking of variances introduced as many errors as it corrected.

		Check counter		
($N_C = 100$, $N = 1400$)		**Correct**	**Incorrect**	**Totals**
Check report	**Correct**	39.3%	17.0%	56.3%
	Incorrect	20.7%	23.0%	43.7%
	Totals	60.0%	40.0%	100%

Figure 18.6: Tidy stock variance check procedure.

For untidy stock about two-thirds of the items identified on the variance report were actually incorrect (66.6%). Also, the total accuracy improvement was only 36.9% and this was offset by the addition of error of 9.2%. Overall the variance report for untidy stock improved accuracy by a modest 2.0% (since $N_c = 100$, $N = 1400$, $b = 9.2$ and $c = 36.9$, where $100 / 1400 \times (36.9\% - 9.2\%) = 2.0\%$).

		Check counter		
($N_c = 100$, $N = 1400$)		Correct	Incorrect	Totals
Check report	Correct	24.2%	9.2%	33.4%
	Incorrect	36.9%	29.7%	66.6%
	Totals	61.1%	38.9%	100%

Figure 18.7: Untidy stock variance check procedure.

18.4 Item checking comparison

Figure 18.8 shows a summary of the improvements in accuracy using reasonability and variance stock count checks. Note that the initial counting stage accuracy was 90% for tidy stock and only 80% for untidy stock.

The best performer was the reasonability check when the stock was untidy. It indicated that correcting obvious counting errors was beneficial and improved inventory accuracy (80% + 3.9% = 83.9%).

The checking of variances with tidy stock was of little value (90% + 0.3% = 90.3%). This suggested that for tidy stock, correcting variance report discrepancies can almost add as much error as it reduces.

Accuracy (%)	Counting stage %	Checking stage %	Final accuracy %
Reasonability tidy	90	2.1	92.1
Reasonability untidy	80	3.9	83.9
Variance tidy	90	0.3	90.3
Variance untidy	80	2.0	82.0

Figure 18.8: Percentage of counting accuracy and checking accuracy using reasonability and variance checks with tidy and untidy stock.

18.5 Item checking duration

Check procedures seek to both find and correct errors which occurred during the stock count. Another important measure of their utility is not just their effectiveness, but also the time required to complete them.

Figure 18.9 shows the average time required to count tidy and untidy stock: 192 and 228 minutes respectively. It also shows the average time needed to check approximately 100 tidy and untidy stock items using reasonability and variance checking strategies.

Most noticeable was that checking 100 items took about the same time as the initial counting stage required. Clearly, the checking procedure was very slow.

Working from the check list, the counter was required to find the listed item on the shelf, count its quantity and confirm whether it matched with the quantity on the list. Sometimes items were found in multiple places within a location. This was a tedious and very slow procedure.

Duration (in minutes)	Counting stage	Checking stage	Final duration
Reasonability tidy	192	157	349
Reasonability untidy	228	166	394
Variance tidy	192	151	343
Variance untidy	228	189	417

Figure 18.9: Average duration in minutes for counting and checking a stock count using reasonability and variance checks with tidy and untidy stock.

It is likely during the checking procedures that counters spent most of their time walking around the store trying to find each item on their list. Procedurally this was quite different to normal stock counting, where each item is counted sequentially, one next to another. The ratio of checking time to counting time was roughly four minutes to one. Clearly, long checking procedures add considerable time and therefore cost to a stock count.

18.6 Laboratory store considerations

In Chapter 17, the types of counting error were examined. In this chapter the merits of checking procedures were examined. Best practice suggests that enterprise stock count accuracy should be 95% or higher.[1] However, without any tolerance counting stage, accuracy rates observed in the laboratory store were surprisingly low: approximately 90% for tidy stock and 80% for untidy stock. Even after implementing checking procedures, the accuracy rates only reached 92% and 84% respectively. A number of factors that may have affected the accuracy rates are considered below.

Error definitions and tolerances
During the laboratory stock counts, inventory error was defined as any quantity difference between two counts of the same item. A less sensitive measure of error could have also been used. For instance,

inventory deviation, which considers the total magnitude of unit differences for all items, would have delivered a higher level of accuracy (see Chapters 13 and 16). Similarly, accuracy rates could have been arbitrarily improved by introducing an error tolerance level. Error rates counting tidy stock decreased from 10% to 7% when a ±5% tolerance was used.

However, the laboratory store research was focused on determining counter performance thresholds using a range of stock types without tolerances. While tolerances can be justified in commercial settings they were not a central interest in the laboratory store.

Number of items

The number and distribution of items in the experimental store may not be representative of all trading enterprises. Certainly a larger store with more and varied items may yield different results. However, having 1400 items counted repeatedly by 81 people provided a large error data set. Different items may yield different base line results, but the relationships between conditions are unlikely to change. It would be useful to establish a larger laboratory store, but such exercises are costly.

Task difficulty

Many items were in small quantities and easily confused, especially for the untidy stock. Apart from their basic training the counters were not informed of potentially difficult areas or instructed to use any specific counting strategies. In this study, those that used AQ1 techniques effectively had the fewest errors.

Good enterprise managers, when supervising a stock count, should identify high-error risk areas and strategies for counting them.

Systematic error

The counters used to establish the laboratory store reference inventory were never used in the preparation, counting or checking stage research. However in the modern enterprise, often the same people use similar processes to prepare, count and check the same stock. If the same people and processes are used for each stage of the stock count there is a risk that the same systematic errors will be made in each stage.

Indeed, in the laboratory store, many counters concurred and allocated the same units for an item that differed vastly in the reference inventory. Examples include dog food (see Figure 17.3) and drink sachets (see Figure 17.7). Using a highly accurate and independent comparator, like the reference inventory, probably highlights many more 'true' errors that would not be detected in less exacting stock count environments.

18.7 Summary

Checking stage

Good stock count practice requires that checks are made during and after the counting stage. Checking finds counting errors and improves overall stock count accuracy. However, any check and recount strategies risk generating their own errors which may actually decrease overall inventory accuracy. There are a number of techniques and strategies for testing and checking the accuracy of the stock count. Three methods were considered here and the results are summarized below.

Location checking

There are two common types of location checks: location completion checks and location unit checks. Location completion checks merely ensure that all locations have been counted. This checking is relatively simple to perform, takes little time and highlights missed or duplicated areas. Finding and correcting a missed location is the easiest way to improve stock count accuracy, since every item in the missed location is an error and recounting it virtually corrects every error.

Location unit checking is where the total units in each location are recounted and compared to the number of stock count items and quantities observed in that location. Location unit checking requires more counter resources and can double the stock count duration. Such checks largely identify gross quantity discrepancies and not specific item identification errors. As such, location unit checking adds little to stock count accuracy.

Item checking

There are many ways to select individual stock count items for checking. Reasonability checks add value to the stock count process. They can be based on management experience, where items often known to be in error are checked, or automatically generated where items within a location with a higher than average quantity are checked.

Variance checking also facilitates inventory accuracy. However, like all checks, the comparative inventory must be accurate if it is to identify errors and avoid consuming valuable time and resources by recounting items that are in fact correct.

19: Sampling stage

In the earlier chapters, inventory accuracy was measured by comparing stock counts of a laboratory store with a known reference inventory. The reference inventory was established by meticulously counting the laboratory stock repeatedly, independently and using different stock counting methodologies, comparing results, and then rechecking and correcting any discrepancies.

This was only possible because the physical stock holding was small and fixed in an experimental setting. Normally enterprises cannot indefinitely suspend trade and fix their stock levels for long periods. Nor can they afford to establish a reference inventory of all stock items by repeated stock counts.

More commonly, only a small random sample of stock items is selected in order to measure inventory accuracy in a trading enterprise. These items are usually counted only once, compared to the inventory of interest, and the number of error discrepancies counted. That is, a sample stock count is used to evaluate the accuracy of another inventory source, typically a perpetual inventory or another full (all items) stock count.

This chapter is largely concerned with the sampling stage of the stock count where, having established a stock count (or perpetual inventory), the enterprise wants to test and measure its accuracy using samples.

Statistically, in order to determine the accuracy of an existing inventory with a maximum level of confidence, one would count and compare all items. Such an exercise is usually not commercially justifiable and therefore a smaller sample stock count is conducted which is intended to fulfill the same purpose. Any sample must meet two criteria: it needs to be representative, and it needs to be sufficiently large.

19.1 Representative and sufficient samples

To be representative a sample must proportionally reflect all of the stock items, not just a select group. When sampling, enterprise managers are often tempted to focus more heavily in critical areas such as departments or items that are essential, have a high value or quantity, or which are prone to theft. This is understandable and reflects their commercial interests, but carries with it a strong risk that the sample will no longer be representative of the entire stock holding.

Sample representation is most simply addressed by ensuring items are chosen randomly and in equal proportions of all types of stock. In so doing, any stock accuracy differences will be represented in the same proportions as they are in the entire population of stock items.

Statistically, the size of the sample required to estimate the accuracy of a stock count depends on three factors: an error margin, a confidence level in this error margin, and the underlying variability of the stock count accuracy itself.

Firstly the enterprise manager must decide what sample error margin will be acceptable. Since the sample stock count is only a portion of the entire population, it is only an estimate of the accuracy of the entire stock count. For example: one cannot state with complete certainty that the initial stock count was, say, 93.4% accurate; but we can state that the initial stock count accuracy was 93.4% ± 2.6%. Such an approach specifies the error range of values that the initial stock count could have had, without specifying what the actual accuracy was (though the mid-point, 93.4%, is often taken to be the most likely value). Smaller error margins will require larger sample sizes.

This approach assumes that the full stock count accuracy lies within this range. This is not always true; however, it is possible—by chance and through no fault of the sampling technique—that a preponderance of accurate items was chosen. Consequently the final accuracy may have appeared better than it was. It is for this reason that enterprise managers must consider their statistical *confidence*, and the probability that the actual accuracy level is found within the error margin.

This is commonly referred to as a 'confidence interval of 95%' or '95% CI'. This means that the true underlying accuracy level for the population will be found within the error margin 95% of the time. Or conversely, the accuracy level will not be found in one out of 20 samples. A confidence interval is a combination of an error margin and a confidence level. It does not specify where in the error margin the true value lies; it could be in the middle, at 93.4% in our example, or closer to the top at 96%, or the bottom at 90.8%. A 99% CI will be wrong (the error margin will not contain the underlying population accuracy rate) about once every 100 times. Greater confidence levels require larger sample sizes.

The final factor which affects the size of the required sample is the underlying variability of the population. If there are a large number of accurate and inaccurate items (say 50% of each) there is high variability and thus a large sample is needed. Given very high accuracy rates, say closer to 99%, there is less variability because all items tend to be accurate and a smaller sample is needed. Higher levels of variability require larger sample sizes.

There are a number of statistical formulae used to calculate sample sizes, given different data assumptions and distributions.[2] When considering stock count accuracy as it is measured here, there are only two possible outcomes. If two counts of the same item agree the item is accurate, and if they disagree the item is in error. This type of data is called 'binomial' (since there are only two alternatives) and assuming it is normally distributed its sample size can be calculated using the following formula:[3,4]

$$n = \frac{z_{\alpha/2}^2 \hat{p}(1 - \hat{p})}{\varepsilon^2}$$

Where:

n is the required sample size

$z_{\alpha/2}$ is the z-score for the confidence level from the standardized normal distribution

$\hat{p}$ is the sample accuracy rate (or an estimate of it)

ε is the error margin

Figure 19.1 provides a table of samples sizes calculated using the above sample size formula. It provides three levels of stock count accuracy (>95%, >80% and for interest, 50%), confidence level (99%, 95%, 80%) and error margin (1%, 3% and 5%). The table serves as a guide to the required sample size to achieve a certain CI, given an estimate of the accuracy rate. If the estimate of the accuracy rate is not correct, the sample can still be used, but the CI will not be as good or bad as expected. An overestimate of the accuracy rate, for example, will lead to a CI that is worse than expected for the intended sample size. For example, if an enterprise manager assumes that the accuracy level of a stock count is likely to be greater than 80% and they would like to achieve a CI of ±3% at the 95% confidence level, they would refer to Figure 19.1 and see that the required sample size is 683. To be conservative and safe, this could be rounded up to 700 items.

	High accuracy >95%			Medium accuracy >80%			Low accuracy = 50%		
Confidence level	99	95	80	99	95	80	99	95	80
Error margin	**Sample size required**								
1%	3162	1825	791	10651	6147	2663	16641	9604	4161
3%	352	203	88	1184	683	296	1849	1068	463
5%	127	73	32	427	246	107	667	385	167

Figure 19.1: Required sample sizes to estimate stock count accuracy, given various error margins and confidence levels.

After the sample stock count has been collected, the CI can be calculated simply by rearranging the above sample size formula to:

$$\varepsilon = \frac{z\alpha/_2 \ \sqrt{\hat{p}(1-\hat{p})}}{\sqrt{n}}$$

Assume for instance, that the accuracy agreement between the sample and full stock counts was 83.4%. The error margin or 95% CI for this value is 2.75% and is calculated below:

$$\varepsilon = \frac{z_{\alpha/2}\sqrt{\hat{p}(1-\hat{p})}}{\sqrt{n}} = \frac{1.96\sqrt{.834(1-.834)}}{\sqrt{700}} = .0275$$

This indicates that the 95% CI for the stock count accuracy is anywhere between 80.6% and 86.2% (83.4% – 2.75% and 83.4% + 2.75%). In other words, there is only a 1 in 20 chance that the true accuracy of the full stock count lays outside this range.

If the enterprise manager wanted a greater confidence than 95% they could increase it to say 99%. However this would have the effect of widening the error margin to 3.62% where:

$$\varepsilon = \frac{z_{\alpha/2}\sqrt{\hat{p}(1-\hat{p})}}{\sqrt{n}} = \frac{2.576\sqrt{.834(1-.834)}}{\sqrt{700}} = .0362$$

In other words, the 99% CI for the stock count accuracy ranges between 79.8% and 87.0%. This means that the full stock count accuracy would fall outside this interval once in about 100 samples.

Sample sizes for accuracy testing

A second purpose of sample size and CI estimation is to test a hypothesis about stock count accuracy. For instance, an enterprise manager might want to test the claim that a stock counting team was 98% accurate. To do so, he would count a representative random sample of stock items and compare them to those of the stock count team. He would then calculate the accuracy and the 95% CI. If the desired 98% fell outside of the calculated CI range the accuracy rate would not be achieved and the hypothesis disproved.

It is important when testing a hypothesis that the desired confidence level and sample size are specified before the sample stock count is conducted. Once that sample has been collected and the error margins (CI) calculated from the observed results, even if the data yields 'unfavorable' results, it is not permissible to simply check another 100 items say, and retest the hypothesis. Doing so just increases the chances of spurious results where the sample is no longer random or representative.

Stratified samples

Statistically, it may be possible to stratify all stock into a number of smaller sub-groups and then randomly sample each sub-group and test its accuracy. For instance, stock may be stratified according to its value, category or risk. Any strata should be mutually exclusive where every item is assigned to only one group. The strata should also be exhaustive where no item of stock is excluded. Statistical stratification can improve the representativeness of each group and thereby reduce sampling error. However, it is a complex area of statistics and care must be taken to apply such techniques.

Further considerations

Statistics are powerful tools, but their use and interpretation depend on important assumptions and care when collecting data. To avoid misleading results and incorrect conclusions, it is clearly essential that any sampled stock count is large enough and representative of the full stock count population. Sampling more higher-value items than low-value items, for instance, says more about the accuracy level of valuable items than it does about the accuracy level of the entire stock count.

When completing stock count accuracy measurement, it is generally assumed that the sample stock count is correct and all observed discrepancies are due to errors in the full stock count. In reality this assumption is unlikely to be correct (see Chapters 13 and 14). There may be several opposing counting errors that affect the reliability of a stock count accuracy sample. For instance:

- Random counting errors when sampling are likely to increase the discrepancy between a full stock count and make the measured accuracy appear lower. They have a conservative effect since they may make accuracy appear lower than it actually is.

- Systematic counting errors where both the full stock count and the sample stock count make the same mistake, but agree. These are likely to make measured accuracy appear higher and therefore can inflate the apparent accuracy.

While these factors may cancel each other out to some extent each may be present during any accuracy measurement.

Clearly measuring stock count accuracy in the field is not easy and much depends on the stock environment, the initial stock counters and the skill of the manager to complete the sample and comparative counts systematically and objectively.

Most surprising is that in order to test stock count accuracy in any statistically conventional way the essential sample size needed is surprising large, typically requiring hundreds of counts. In practice few enterprise managers or auditors have the time or resources to actually complete this task. Indeed, in reality, many reported measures of stock count accuracy, especially those based on small and unrepresentative samples, are quite possibly incorrect.

19.2 Summary

Sample assumptions

A sample stock count can be conducted to compare to a full stock count in order to gauge its accuracy. While the underling accuracy can differ from the apparent agreement rate, in the absence of more information, they are conservatively assumed to be equal.

Sample sizes

To ensure a correct and meaningful result, the sample must be:

- sufficiently large so that it reflects the underlying variance of the stock environment, the accuracy rate's error margin, and the level of confidence of the error margin

- representative of all stock (otherwise more sophisticated stratified sampling techniques are intending to be used)
- completed diligently to minimize additional spurious counting errors.

V: Notes

1   Kutz, Gregory. *Executive Guide: Best Practice in Achieving Consistent, Accurate Physical Counts of Inventory and Related Property*. Washington: United States General Accounting Office, 2002.

       Brooks, Roger B. and Wilson, Larry W. *Inventory Record Accuracy*. Hoboken, New Jersey: John Wiley & Sons, 2007.

2   *Problem Solvers Statistics*, Research and Education Association, USA, 2007.

3   Cochran, William G. *Sampling Techniques*, 2nd ed. New York, John Wiley & Sons, 1963.

4   Lohr, Sharon L. *Sampling: Design and Analysis*, Pacific Grove, USA, Brooks Cole Publishing, 1999.

PART VI: BEST PRACTICE

20: Policies and methods

This section examines the best-practice stock count policies and methods in light of research and documented experience. It also examines the future of the stock count, given emerging technologies.

Consider this surprisingly common scenario:

> Customers are complaining that our warehouse is sending them
> the wrong stock. Our warehouse locations and stock are sometimes
> poorly marked, consequently our people confuse the stock and units
> and people stow and pick the wrong stock. This causes anomalies in
> our computer system's perpetual inventory. So we need an urgent
> stock count to get a 100% accurate inventory to fix our problems.
> We plan to get it counted tonight.

Before engaging in a stock count the enterprise must get its house in order. The role of the stock count is to measure the physical stock—its location, items and quantity. The stock count cannot fix poorly marked and unidentifiable stock. Indeed, the accuracy of the stock count will be affected by the nature of the stock, its environment and the people who count it. Without addressing the broader stock identification issues an accurate inventory will be impossible.

20.1 Stock count policies

Frequency and budget
Frequency and budget vary widely across industries and circumstances. Not surprisingly, enterprises that enforce good stock management policies are typically the same that insist on regular

independent stock counts. Best-practice enterprises reportedly complete between one and four full stock counts each year and use periodic cyclic stock counts, especially in troublesome areas, throughout the year.[1]

Management team

It is essential that inventory managers are accountable with defined performance goals. Stock count policies should articulate those in charge of the process, and the metrics used to determine their performance, including the desired levels of accuracy. Common metrics include defined levels of inventory accuracy, shrinkage, pick rates and so on.[2]

Documentation

All well-run enterprises that provide good stock management include documentation of 'inventory procedures' or 'stocktake manuals'. Enterprises often write standardized stock count polices that dictate the method used and the frequency of stock counts. If available, handheld devices are used in preference to stock sheets. Reports compare the stock count with a corresponding perpetual inventory. Lastly, human resources are chosen from their own employees or from an external inventory service provider. Included in the manual are accuracy definitions, tolerances, counting, checking and sampling policies.

Purpose

The stock count procedures will vary depending on the purpose of the stock count. If the count is merely to generate a valuation, the stock need only be counted for each price point and not each item number level. Recall that traditionally, financial inventories were those where the stock was not separated into unique items but counted and valued at its retail price point to save time (see Chapter 3). On the other hand, if the stock count is to be compared to a perpetual inventory then it must be counted at the same item level as recorded in the perpetual inventory. Lastly, if the stock count is to be used to verify a planogram, data collection may need to include counting of the data at each location, facing, item and quantity.

Sourcing people

Stock counters are people and they bring to the task different levels of motivation, ability and experience. Some will be faster and more accurate than others. In addition, counter speed and accuracy is likely to increase as experience is garnered.

Another major policy decision concerns the source of people to count the stock. The enterprise can choose to use its own employees, an external service provider or a combination of the two. Arguments supporting the use of internal employees include that they:

- are more familiar with the stock and therefore more accurate
- are cheaper because there is no third-party profit margin
- have people at all sites (even remote ones) that can complete the stock counts on the same day.

Arguments in favor of using independent service providers include that they:

- are cheaper when a full analysis of all internal costs is made
- use best-practice technology and procedures and are more accurate and efficient
- are convenient and available when needed, freeing employees to focus on other core functions
- are trained professionals that are independent and objective.

Obviously the enterprise must complete a thorough analysis to truly resolve these issues. The fact that all of the largest retailers throughout the Americas and Europe use independent service providers adds further credibility to outsourcing.

Cyclic versus full stock counts

Although cyclic and full stock counts have slightly different advantages and disadvantages, their concepts and methods are fundamentally the same. Many organizations use a mixture of the two as part of their planned inventory management strategy.

Full stock counts are generally preferred by auditors as they provide a most transparent review of the stock and are independent of the perpetual inventory (see Chapter 7).

On the other hand, cyclic stock counts are useful to maintain high levels of perpetual accuracy in troublesome areas. The fact that stock count error rates vary widely across different departments highlights the value of cyclic stock counts. Troublesome areas can be counted more regularly to ensure better overall accuracy (see Chapter 7).

Recall that a cyclic stock count is not the same as a diagnostic error check, since it does not represent a random sample from all stock items, but rather 100% of a selected area. As such, cyclic stock counts can provide confidence in the perpetual stock but they are not likely to be statistically representative of all stock.

Measures of accuracy

It is vital, in order to accurately maintain an inventory, that all the assumptions and consequences implicit in the definition of accuracy are understood. There are two main options available to an enterprise manager in order to measure the accuracy of the inventory. One measures the number of item-level errors and the other measures the magnitude of item-quantity deviations (see Chapter 13).

Inventory error is defined as the number of item-quantity discrepancies greater than a predetermined tolerance. Accuracy is the difference between all items and the number of errors and can be expressed as a percentage relative to all items.

Considerable thought needs to be given to any tolerances that are used. Individual item tolerances are time-consuming to maintain, whereas applying a general one (like 5% for all stock) may be too crude.

It is common to define inventory deviation as the sum of the absolute item-quantity discrepancies and express it as a percentage relative to the total item units. Measures of deviation based on quantity or stock value show higher levels of accuracy than merely counting item discrepancies (see Chapter 13).

Inventory deviation measures are weighted by the magnitude of the quantity discrepancy. Large deviations imply large item-quantity errors. However, if item quantities are themselves large, deviation discrepancies tend to appear even smaller as a proportion of the total quantity. For instance, in big box retail environments where item quantities have thousands of units, inventory accuracy measures can reach 99%, since deviations are small relative to the large unit quantities found in the store.

Measures of productivity

Stock count accuracy is a function of time. If more time is spent diligently preparing and counting the stock then accuracy is likely to be higher (see Chapter 14). A widely-used measure of speed is the average units counted per hour (often abbreviated to 'average per hour' or APH). APH simply represents the number of units counted, divided by the number of hours taken to count it. If the total quantity of all items is 2000 and it took 2.5 hours to count these units, then the APH is 800 (2000/2.5).

APH will naturally vary depending on the type of stock and its preparation. The exact methods used to calculate APH may also vary. Some adjustments and treatment may be made to parameters that affect the calculation of the stock count duration. For instance, APH may include or exclude:

- rest and meal breaks
- counter only or counter and supervisor time
- preparation or checking time
- all stock or selective stock.

As long as the method of calculation is used consistently and where possible influential parameters are controlled, APH is a valuable tool to measure and distinguish stock count performance across counters, sites or preparation levels.

Good stock count practice provides counters with performance feedback during and after the course of the stock count.[3] APH indicates relative productivity and can be used to compare counters or performance in similar stock environments. For instance, the APH in a book store where a large proportion of items are barcode-scanned individually may vary from around 600 to 900. By contrast, a supermarket with an average item quantity of around 10 will have an APH nearer 2000.

Acceptable accuracy level

Thorough stock count procedures will generate higher levels of accuracy, but at a cost. Insisting that every item be removed from its box and stacked before counting might improve stock count accuracy slightly, but the stock count duration might increase five-fold (see Chapter 14). Stock count accuracy (and precision) comes at a price, but it must be commercial. Enterprise managers must choose a procedure that will give them an adequate level of accuracy for an affordable price. When a new stock count procedure is trialed, its accuracy should be sampled and measured to determine if it meets the enterprise's accuracy requirements and its budget.

20.2 Technology and equipment

Stock sheets

Procedurally, stock counts are commonly conducted using either stock sheets or handheld devices. The merits of each of these methods are considered below.

Choose the stock count method well in advance. If stock sheets are to be used, print a sample and check that they are representative of all stock. If handheld devices are used, conduct a mock stock count and ensure that all computer hardware and software work properly and operators are familiar with it. A stock count is a snapshot in time. If it is not used to update computer records in a timely fashion it is of little value.

Before the existence of computers, itemized stock counts were completed using stock sheets. These were handwritten with the stock details such as the stock number or description, location, price and quantity. Today many computerized perpetual stock systems support both stock sheet and handheld stock count facilities. The stock sheets are printed before the stock count. Ideally they are page numbered and are printed in the order in which the stock resides by location on the shelf. This makes finding each item within the stock sheets a little easier than a mere numeric or alphabetically arranged list.

The stock counters use these sheets to direct them to the location. They then verify that the stock observed on the sheet matches that in the location, count the observed stock quantity and record it on the stock sheet. The completed stock sheet is subsequently keypunched into a perpetual stock system. The computer system automatically compares the stock count and stock-on-hand data and generates a variance report indicating any discrepancies. Any variances are checked and where necessary, corrections made. The checked stock count data is then used to update the perpetual inventory.

While the use of stock sheets is common in many enterprise environments, they have a number of shortcomings:

- Stock sheets frequently get lost, dirty and are often illegible after written additions and corrections.
- Quantities are handwritten and may be difficult to read. Arithmetic is usually completed mentally or with workings written on the sheet.
- Stock sheets assume the only stock to count is observed on the stock sheets in the specified location; stock on the shelf but not listed on the stock sheet is easily missed.
- Stock sheets require the counter(s) to identify the stock item number and search for the corresponding stock sheet item number. This is error-prone and time-consuming.
- Stock sheets encourage counters to work efficiently in pairs: one counting and the other searching and recording the count details. This may arguably be more accurate, if each checks and

confirms the stock count, but often one handles the stock to count it and the other merely records the count.

- Stock sheets must be preprinted and subsequently manually key-punched. Keypunching the data requires another level of human data processing that may increase stock count errors. Handheld devices can transfer data to other computers instantly with an exceedingly low probability of data loss.

Handheld devices

Handheld devices are essentially portable computers with a built-in barcode reader, screen, central processor, electronic memory, data entry keyboard, communication ports, and battery power supply (see Chapter 12). Many enterprises' perpetual stock systems support handheld devices for electronic stock count data entry.

All leading inventory service providers who perform stock counts commercially on a large scale use handheld devices in preference to stock sheets or other technology. The main advantages of handheld devices in the stock count process include:

- Fast and reliable item searching. Instead of the counter searching through a list of stock sheet items, a handheld device can auto-matically search the verification inventory for the item. This is faster, less error-prone and less fatiguing for the counter.
- Single data entry on-site. The counter finds the items and enters the count at the stock location. By contrast, stock sheets require handwritten counts which are later interpreted and keypunched, often by others.
- Counters work individually. This is in contrast to stock sheets, which encourage counters to work in pairs, often with only one counting. Counters using handheld devices are faster and more independent.
- Stock location driven process. The stock count flow follows the physical stock in its location and not the order of stock as it appears on the stock sheets. Consequently, stock is less likely to be missed.

- Faster preparation and completion. The stock count is not delayed by the printing of stock sheets. Completed reports can be also printed immediately after the count is finished, without the need to keypunch stock sheets.
- Additional features. Handheld devices may provide the counter with visual or audible warnings if stock is unusual in some way; for instance, if it is in an unexpected location, a non-standard pack size, and so on. Many provide calculator features to assist with arithmetic.

Some shortcomings are that handheld devices are more costly than stock sheets and require specialized software and some training to establish their use. For these reasons in small stock count situations, stock sheets may still be an easier and cheaper solution. Also, in parts of the world where the cost of labor is very cheap and technology limited, stock sheets may be commercially more affordable.

Equipment
Equipment is a vital part of the stock count effort. Scales can be used to count physically small items with large units and low value; however, they need to be regularly calibrated to confirm their accuracy. Ideally, this should be done annually.

In a warehouse setting, pallets with mixed stock need to be brought to the ground using forklifts and unpacked for counting. However, single stock types in clearly marked boxes can often be counted in situ and accessed using scissor lifts.

Safety ladders, harnesses and other such stock access equipment all facilitate accuracy if they make the counting of the stock faster, easier and safer.

20.3 Reporting

Some enterprises have over 50 stock count reports, however many of these merely provide the same information in a variety of formats. A useful list of reports that serve most enterprise requirements is outlined below. These are arranged into two categories: check reports and summary reports. Check reports serve to facilitate the checking of the stock count process at an item level whereas summary reports provide consolidated stock count information.

Check report: Itemized handheld device report

This report lists each counter's stock count data in the exact sequence and units that it was counted. It will include the counter, location and start/finish time to highlight productivity. It is an excellent report that can be easily checked against the physical stock to determine how a counter is performing.

Check report: Variance report

This report lists discrepancies between a stock count and another stock record, usually the perpetual stock count. Fields included are item number, description, location, stock value (e.g. cost, retail), verification inventory quantity, stock count quantity and their difference. Ideally it will be sorted electronically and can be printed in at least three different data sequence formats:

- item number order, where for each item the stock-on-hand and stock count locations are individually listed and the total stock summed and reconciled. This clearly indicates where any item of stock can be found, across multiple locations
- location (bin) number order, where every site location is listed in order with the stock-on-hand and stock count item numbers. This makes moving through the site in location order and checking stock quantities very easy
- variance magnitude, where discrepancies are listed in value or quantity order. This report easily identifies the major stock count discrepancies.

Check report: Reasonability report

This report lists items that are worthy of checking because of their unusual nature and the likelihood of stock count errors. Some examples are:

- items within a location with a stock count quantity twice the average quantity in that location
- 200 items with the largest stock quantity
- 100 items with the largest stock value.

Ideally it can be sorted electronically and printed in several different data sequence formats:

- Stock item number order, where for each item the stock-on-hand and stock count locations are individually listed and the total stock summed and reconciled. This clearly indicates where any item of stock can be found, across multiple locations.
- Location (bin) number order, where every location in the warehouse is listed in order with the stock-on-hand and stock count item numbers. This makes moving through the warehouse in location order and checking stock quantities very easy.

Check report: Not found item listing report

This report lists any items observed in the verification inventory that were not observed in the stock count. It can be useful where the number of items in the verification inventory is close to the actual items observed in the stock count and will highlight any missed items. If the verification file is very large, perhaps including many seasonal or items that are no longer stocked, it can be of little value.

Check report: All items report

This report lists each item of stock (usually item number, description and quantity). Typically it is printed in stock department and item description order. Often it will be collapsed over item number where each unique item number only appears once.

Other check reports

There are many other reports that can be of use, but they are industry-specific. In particular, any stock item parameter that is stored in an electronic format can be compared to the stock count data and a report generated. For instance, in book retailing, within a defined time period, certain unsold books can be returned to the publisher without charge.

Physically finding these books among thousands can be difficult and slow. However, immediately after a stock count, where everything is counted, these books can be more easily identified. A specific report can be generated listing each of the books subject to return that were observed in the stock count. The report lists each book for returning, including its quantity, location and even where within a location it can be found (beginning, middle or end). This makes the subsequent picking of these books much faster and easier.

Another useful selected report, often used by retailers, lists stock only found in the store room that is not observed on the shop floor. Obviously, stock held only in the storage reflects significant holding costs. Perhaps the stock is seasonal and will be displayed later in the year, but often it is simply forgotten and needs to be addressed.

The power to generate selected reports also helps the checking of the stock count. Item lists of random locations or selected stock counts can be printed for ease of checking. Also, high-risk areas that are difficult to count or prone to shrinkage can be printed for additional review.

Summary report: Location

This report lists the total stock value or total stock quantity for each location. The definition of a location is arbitrary. It may consist of a warehouse stock bin with only one or two unique items, or more commonly around 100 items found on a shelving fixture and defined only temporarily for a stock count (see Chapter 11). The report can merely list each location or a hierarchy of locations with totals for each level. The location summary highlights missed or duplicated locations.

Summary report: Department

This report lists the total stock value or total stock quantity for each enterprise category or department. It will often include totals for a second inventory such as the perpetual stock count. A hierarchy of departments can all be used such as a category (grocery) and subcategory (dry goods, frozen, dairy). The department report can be used to summarize the stock value at cost or retail and any discrepancies between it and the perpetual stock value.

Summary report: Counter

This report is largely a productivity report of each person physically counting the stock. It can list each counter's start and finish times, the locations and total units that they counted. Summary statistics can also be included, like APH or any of their counts that were corrected during the count checking process.

20.4 Verification file

Stock count speed and accuracy depends to a large extent on the nature of stock, its preparation and environment. However, a further factor affecting stock count accuracy is the veracity of the inventory used to verify the stock item numbers and details as they are collected. Recall that all modern stock counts use either stock sheets or handheld devices to collect stock count data. Normally a perpetual stock system is used to generate and print stock sheets or an electronic stock list that is loaded into handheld devices. This verification inventory will influence the speed and manner in which the stock count data is collected.

For instance, stock items observed on the shelf but not found in the verification inventory will confuse and delay their accurate counting. Items with poor or incorrect stock descriptions will also confuse counters, leading to a slower stock count with more error. Worse, stock with mismatching item numbers and descriptions in the verification inventory are already in error and may not be detected or corrected during the course of the stock count.

In summary, an item unambiguously distinguished from its background is more likely to be accurately counted. People can count reliably and quickly, but they cannot always correctly identify item numbers and stock. Recall that in the laboratory store study, 96% of counters accurately counted nine cans of dog food during a stock count. However, less than 50% allocated the correct quantity to its corresponding item number. Stock that is not easily identified, due to its nature or the environment is prone to stock count error (see Chapter 17).

Below is a short summary of common factors affecting the verification inventory (using stock sheets or handhelds):

- same item number with different item descriptions
- item numbers without descriptions
- item numbers without corresponding barcodes
- incorrect barcodes
- inconsistent, short, ambiguous, misspelled item descriptions.

20.5 Summary

Stock count policies

To be able to conduct fast and accurate stock counts, best-practice dictates that polices are documented and administered. Stock count policy and method documentation should include:

- frequency and budget guidelines
- accountable managers with performance goals
- definitions including accuracy and productivity measures and targets
- clear and enforceable procedures and reporting
- available technology including handheld devices, stock access equipment and current verification file
- stock counter requirements and guidelines.

21: Stock count stages

Having examined best-practice stock count policies and methods in the previous chapter, this chapter examines best practices across the four stages of the stock count in light of research and documented experience.

21.1 Preparing stage

The nature of the stock, its neatness and preparedness for counting affect the speed and accuracy with which it can be counted. Indeed, fast and accurate stock counting depends as much on good stock preparation as it does on the competence of the stock counter.

The stock arrangement can certainly be structured to facilitate stock identification. Only accessible stock, neatly arranged and clearly marked, is conducive to high levels of stock count accuracy.[4]

This reasoning is supported experimentally, where stock count error increased by 200% when stock was untidily arranged (see Chapter 16). Below is a short summary of common stock factors that make stock identification more difficult, increasing the likelihood of identification count error.

Stock
- specialized stock requiring high levels of specific stock knowledge
- indistinguishable stock varieties and packaging
- inconsistent stock packaging and units (pairs, dozens, gift packs, bonus packs, etc.).

Environment

- adverse lighting, noise, temperature, weather, height and cleanliness
- limited or poor stock access
- incorrect item number labels and item descriptions
- uncalibrated scales used to weigh and count items
- many to one locations, making item reconciliation across locations difficult
- similar stock varieties in the same location
- new and used stock together (such as working and in need of repair)
- closed boxes with more than one open box
- unorganized and excessively large stock units
- unclear stock cut-offs and period-ends
- poorly arranged and mixed items
- poorly defined stock count and quarantine areas
- unmarked partially full boxes mixed with full boxes
- stacked boxes with inconsistent stock units stored in each.

Basic stock count procedures are largely commonsense. Well-faced and clearly labeled stock is easily identified, facilitating stock count speed and accuracy. By contrast, handwritten labels inconsistently placed on shelving or items, with ad hoc and inconsistent stock locations, cultivates misinterpretation and counting error.

Stock preparation includes:

- items arranged together neatly
- stock varieties arranged together and demarcated from other like items
- full boxes stacked together
- only one item number per box
- stock items and shelves clearly labeled.

If there are no formal stock bins or location numbers, systematically apply a sequential location number to each fixture and stock area. Location numbers help guide the stock count. Missing or duplicated location numbers highlight count errors and facilitate accuracy. Location numbered floor plans also help to monitor the flow of the stock count. As areas are systematically allocated and counted, the stock counter and time can be marked off on the floor plan.[5]

Stock cut-offs

Enterprises must ensure that stock cut-offs are accurate. Items or areas that do not need or require counting need to be quarantined and well-marked. A late delivery, emergency stock pick or unprocessed paperwork can create discrepancies between the expected verification stock inventory and the physical stock. All sales, purchases and transfers needed to be recorded in the perpetual stock system in order to synchronize with the physical stock in situ.[6]

21.2 Counting stage

The stock count process consists of the methods used to identify, count and record the stock. Computer technology (handheld devices, scales, etc.) facilitates fast stock identification, counting and recording. However, it does not replace human intelligence to choose the right item and to count it correctly. At all times the counter must scan or keypunch an item number, and then count which items belong with that item number. Even if they are not counting and merely scanning each individual item, counters must ensure that each item is scanned only once and that items are not missed. An error in any step will lead to one or more errors in the inventory.

Novices versus experienced counters

Experienced stock counters are faster that novices, but if the stock is mixed and poorly arranged they may not be more accurate. Good counting techniques are only beneficial when stock is neat and well prepared.

There is no correlation between an individual's stock counting rates and their corresponding accuracy rates. A fast stock counter is not necessarily an accurate one, and vice-versa (see Chapter 17).

If the counter is asked to collect more than three fields during a stock count, their cognitive performance will naturally suffer. Item number, quantity and location, or item number, quantity and retail, are cognitively achievable tasks and commonly required, but speed and accuracy will deteriorate enormously if more concurrent tasks are added (see Chapter 4).

Cognitive load

People's cognitive ability is limited. Their basic numeracy is established at an early age through education. It is important to motivate, yet not fatigue or overload them with cognitive effort. If the counters are given too many extra tasks and exceptions, they are likely to make frequent mistakes and work more slowly. This is not because they cannot count; rather it is because the stock count preparation and process are inadequate and tax the limits of the stock counter (see Chapter 4).

Counter numbers and timing

Timing is critical to the success of a stock count. Too few counters and the stock count takes too long. Counters will become fatigued and need regular breaks. Too many counters and the task will be inefficient and unnecessarily costly. Counter productivity will vary widely and depend on their experience, the nature of the stock and the environment. Exceptionally slow counters, even if highly accurate, are probably not commercially viable and should be avoided. Very fast counters are possibly not counting properly and their work should be checked closely. In short, performance extremes should be monitored and verified.

Stock count task and training

Brief all counters about the process. Physically spot-check their first counted areas to confirm that they have absolutely understood the task, are working effectively and can count accurately.

Most stock count processes using a handheld device only require the counter to:

- record the stock location at the start of a section
- scan or keypunch an item number
- count and record the stock quantity
- mark the completed location before continuing to a new location.

This level of cognitive load is acceptable, but the addition of further tasks will exhaust attention and merely increase the likelihood of counting and identification errors. Additional tasks during a stock count to be avoided are:

- keypunching using different item number formats for different items
- marking each item with a sticker as it is counted
- identifying stock that is damaged, obsolete or expired
- collecting additional data such as an age code, serial number, additional bin number, or retail price
- measuring stock lengths in meters or weighing stock
- moving, tidying, repacking or folding stock
- checking and/or verifying stock item descriptions.

Some of the methods used by experienced counters to achieve high count rates include:

- learning to recognize and distinguish product varieties and package units
- single-scanning low quantities that are difficult to distinguish
- studying the fixture to identify obscured items, hidden drawers, etc.
- counting by eye and avoiding unnecessary touching or handling of the stock
- counting in multiples of two, three, four and so on to avoid counting one item at a time
- knowing and using all arithmetic tables including and above the 12 x 12 table
- using handheld devices and keyboards to enter data without looking at the screen or keys.

Keep the count instructions simple and ensure that there are few procedural exceptions that confuse counters or undermine speed and accuracy. Consider the following written instructions:

> Barcode scan and count everything, except items without a barcode and then key punch the shelf number. Count everything in single units except items marked with a blue label. These are not to be counted. All stock is boxed in units of ten except certain unmarked boxes ...

Is it any wonder that people get confused and make mistakes? Stock count procedural exceptions are hard to remember and implement. Some counters will remember the rule and others will not. Some may misunderstand the rule and happily perform the wrong action. Often management will never know if the exception has been followed, since it occurs randomly and infrequently. Procedural exceptions are to be avoided and reflect bad preparation.

Ambiguous items in small quantities are more accurately counted individually. Items such as clothes, books and wines often look the same but may have different sizes, editions or vintages and therefore have unique item numbers. To avoid confusion when using barcode reading handheld devices, counters should scan each item individually rather than relying on their ability to identify which items are unique.

AQ1 versus KQn

Handheld software can be configured for different methods of item number and quantity data entry. AQ1 (automatic quantity of 1) is where an item number is keypunched or barcode-scanned into the handheld devices and a quantity of 1 is automatically stored. This means the rapid entry of item details as quickly as items are scanned. KQn (keyed quantity greater than 0) is where an item number is keypunched or barcode-scanned into the handheld devices and any quantity is then keypunched into the handheld.

Items such as clothes and books—which can be superficially similar but fundamentally different—are easily confused during a stock count. Stock count managers can use their experience to identify the most effective scanning method when counting such items.

Research suggested that for quantities less than 5, AQ1 scanning was 30% slower than KQn scanning, but up to 10 times more accurate (see Chapter 17).

21.3 Checking stage

Any initial stock count will have some error, probably between 5% and 20% depending on the stock preparation, the counter competence and the count process. The stock count checking procedures are the best opportunity to increase accuracy and perhaps halve stock count error.

The best checks identify items with a high probability of error. Unfortunately, much time is lost walking to the stock location and physically finding the stock on the shelf. Poor checks are those that waste time and resources by suggesting items for checking that when checked, prove to be correct.

Location completion checks

Good stock count practice requires all fixtures and stock areas to be separated into individual locations, areas or bays. Such locations are labeled before the stock count and marked-off as they are counted. Location completion checks identify any locations that were missed or duplicated during the stock count. Such locations are all errors, so finding and correcting them improves relative accuracy enormously.

Location unit checks

Location unit checking is where the number of units in a location is counted and compared to the stock counter's total units. Unfortunately, it has a number of shortcomings:

- it can take almost as long to complete a location unit count as it does to stock count each item and unit
- it only indentifies miscounted stock and not missed or misallocated stock
- it requires all items in a location to be re-counted, when only a one or a few items may be in error.

For these reasons it is of little value as a location checking procedure.

Reasonability checks

Item quantities that are checked because they look unlikely to be correct are called reasonability checks. They are an effective check since they detect a large proportion of errors in a modest amount of time. For instance, a reasonability check completed in the laboratory store required 7% of all items to be recounted and improved stock count accuracy by up to 3.8% (see Chapter 18).

Common reasonability checks include:

- items and/or units in the opinion of an experienced manager that look improbable
- items that historically are prone to confusion and counting error
- items within a location whose quantities differ (too many or too few) from the majority or items in that location
- items with a quantity or valuation that looks improbable (e.g. 111111 or 777).

Variance checks

Variance checks are usually generated when comparing a stock count to a perpetual inventory. Often only large item discrepancies are checked in accordance with a set tolerance value or quantity.

If the perpetual inventory is very inaccurate, checking variances may actually increase overall stock count error. However, many items may be checked that are already correct, wasting time. Also, only discrepant items will be checked; other similar items below the tolerance will not appear on the variance report and can be missed altogether. To illustrate, a variance check completed in the laboratory store required 7% of all items to be recounted and improved stock count accuracy by less than 2% (see Chapter 18).

21.4 Sampling stage

Once a stock count is completed (preparation, counting and checking) management may want to determine its achieved accuracy. This last step has been called 'sampling'.

Any inventory such as a stock count or perpetual inventory can be tested to see if it is accurate. Samples of the physical stock, location, items and quantity can be counted and compared to the comparative inventory. It is recognized that both the sample stock count and the comparative inventory both have errors, but a conservative view is taken and it is accepted that any discrepancy is attributed to the comparative inventory.

Understanding sample sizes

When an estimate is being obtained of how well a given stock count process was performed, it is necessary to take a sample of the recorded counts, and to evaluate the accuracy of these. In order to get a reliable estimate of the accuracy, it is necessary to choose an appropriate sample and sample size.

The sample has to be representative of the stock count performed. If the stock count only included high-value items in a warehouse, such as televisions, it would be inappropriate to then only test one bay of a specific manufacturer's televisions in order to estimate the accuracy of the stock count. An obvious consequence is that if the stock count was conducted over the entire store, then it would be necessary for the sample to be taken from stock across the entire store.

Too small a sample is also useless. In order to get a reasonably good (95% CI) ±5% estimate of our accuracy rate, then it is preferable to obtain samples of at least several hundred items (say 300); the more the better.

21.5 Summary

Preparing stage

Stock count accuracy depends as much on good stock preparation as it does on the stock count process and the counter's competence. Neat, accessible stock, demarcated areas and correct cut-offs can halve the number of stock count errors.

Counting stage

People can count, but they struggle to distinguish between items. If asked to do too many tasks, their accuracy will suffer. Generally,. using a handheld device and scanning individual items (AQ1) is significantly more accurate for small stock quantities less than about five units.

Checking stage

Reasonability and variance checks improve accuracy, but given the time they require, their value is limited. Depending on the nature of the stock, location checks can take as long as the stock count itself and not add much accuracy.

Sampling stage

To actually measure stock count accuracy, a comparative inventory based on a large random sample is required. In practice this is often not completed and consequently many reported measures of accuracy are probably incorrect. Many hundreds of items need to be diligently counted and compared in order to achieve a statistically meaningful measure of accuracy.

22: Future directions

Inventory management requires an unusual mixture of people, technology and process. Surprisingly, technological developments such as the barcode and handheld devices have not decreased the need for accurate stock counts, but rather increased them. The computer and the perpetual inventory have enabled the enterprise to better manage its stock. Informed and accurate stock measurement has led to optimized stock levels, saving the enterprise space, time and money.

However, with more critical stock tolerances, stock count accuracy is essential and the need to measure the stock—the stock count—more frequently required. These days a combined schedule of full and cyclic stock counts is the norm. Certainly multiple stock counts cost more than just one annual count, but these are offset by security and optimization savings.

While the nature of the stock and people are not likely to change in the future, advances in technology will bring further stock count time, cost savings and accuracy improvements.

22.1 Diagnostics on the handheld device

Stock count sampling, where sample counts are made and compared to the stock count to determine a measure of accuracy, are often completed using stock sheets. This is awkward since it takes time to consolidate and compare the data. Also, there may be a tendency to choose an unrepresentative sample or an inadequate size.

A more efficient method is to use sampling software on the handheld device that controls the accuracy measurement process. Consider this method:

- At the completion of a stock count the data is combined (location, item and quantity for all items) and transferred to one or more handheld devices. Additional data like item prices and stock accuracy tolerances can also be included.
- The enterprise management predetermines a conservative estimated accuracy rate, error margin, and level of statistical confidence. Using this information (see Chapter 18) the handheld software calculates the required sample size needed to generate a test of the stock count accuracy.
- The program then randomly chooses locations and items that need to be counted. The stock counter moves to each location and counts the required items and quantities.
- After the sampling is completed and stored in the handheld device, the program automatically compares the sample items with the stock count items. It then calculates and reports the stock count error rate using selected tolerances and deviation measures based on quantity or stock value.

This method formalizes and controls the process of stock count accuracy measurement. RGIS is developing such systems as it ensures a more statistically sound and representative method to measure stock count accuracy.

22.2 Visual stock counts

Merchandising computer systems have long provided visual representations of stock. Floor plans indicating numbered fixtures (locations) can represent a site and its stock distribution across the floor space. Heat maps present any variables linked to the location numbers and display them using shades or colors (see Chapter 3).

RGIS™ has developed a similar system using computerized floor plans illustrating the stock fixtures. As stock is counted, each location on the floor plan is updated and its color changed. For instance, red fixtures represent uncounted locations, amber fixtures represent locations that are being counted and green represents locations fully counted. Other colors represent checked areas, quarantined areas and so on.

The use of the floor plan and real-time heat maps provide a visual representation of the progress of the stock count. This is far more intuitive and meaningful than lists of locations or hand-drawn floor plans. Missed locations are immediately identified by color on a site floorplan. Other variables can also be presented, like using colored fixtures to represent the areas counted by each stock counter. Diagnostic checks such as accuracy rates in different locations can also be displayed easily.

22.3 RFID stock counts

An electronic barcode reading device can only read barcodes that are within its line of site, orientated correctly and a short distance away. For instance, POS check-outs generally require the operator to pass the barcode-marked stock within a foot (300mm) facing the reader. Naturally, it takes time for the POS operator to handle each item of stock through a check-out. This costs money, delays the sale and delays the waiting customer.

One promising way to overcome poor stock identification and slow count speed is the use of RFID tags. RFID tags can be read virtually instantly from any orientation over distances of three feet (one meter) or more.

In regard to the stock count, the RFID tag has the potential to make the stock counter obsolete. RFID readers strategically mounted around the stock environment could, in theory, count all stock in range in seconds, whenever needed, without physically touching the stock.

The widespread implementation of highly accurate, reliable and cheap mobile detection technology, such as might be provided by a future generation of RFID tags, is enormously appealing. Although the technology has been widely available for decades and has enormous promise, it is yet to really take-off in the retail setting. Manufacture costs, reliability and implementation issues remain impediments to its wide-scale use.[7]

In regard to cost, a search on the internet reveals numerous price comparisons and estimates. Passive RFID tags are available for less than US$0.2 each. RFID tag pricing suffers from a common 'chicken and egg' problem. In order to improve the technology, establish economies of scale and generate lower manufacture costs, more enterprises must use the technology. However, enterprises will not use the technology unless the price drops. Certainly in recent years the price has continued to fall, not just of tags, but also the readers and related network infrastructure. Presumably, eventually price will not be an obstacle.

Reliability is also improving, but there remain technical and physical issues. While tag failure is rare, the number, orientation, distance between tags and distance from tag to reader all can cause tags to be undetected. Also the tag environment is a factor. Liquids, metals, grounding, blocking, and reflection can also reduce tag reading reliability. Read failure effectively means lost stock (false negatives) which can undermine stock management and inventory accuracy.

There also remain implementation issues. Computer systems must be modified to accommodate the increased speed and volume of data. For instance, in order to distinguish between items, each unit of stock must be marked with a unique RFID number. Therefore hardware and databases must be much larger to maintain and support the increased number of inventory records.

Ultimately, it is likely that these issues will be resolved and RFID will become a more common stock labeling system. At such time, stock counts will be faster, cheaper and more frequent. However, even then it is likely that independent counters will still be needed to sample, reconcile and test that the physical stock observed actually matches the RFID data recorded in the inventory. Merely detecting a pile of RFID tags does not prove the stock actually physically exists. An independent person or system will still be needed to verify that the stock is present.

22.4 Summary

Stock count accuracy is of value to an enterprise and it can be bought. Good stock management, adequate stock preparation, regular stock counts and modern procedures can ensure high levels of inventory accuracy. However, this all costs time, money and effort to establish. The smart enterprise manager understands this and chooses stock count procedures and accuracy levels that compliment the underlying enterprise.

Until the stock count is completely automated, people will be needed to count the physical stock to verify its existence. People often assumed that when the barcode was introduced, stock counts using people would cease. Somehow the barcode would provide high levels of accuracy that negated the need for the stock count. Similar predictions were made with the introduction of perpetual inventory systems.

In reality, the opposite occurred: the barcode and the perpetual inventory system provide a better and more accurate way to record and manage stock. This has meant that stock levels could be optimized and lowered, generating efficiencies and saving money. However, with lower stock levels, tolerances for error are much lower. Even small counting errors can lead to stock outages with lost sales and missed deadlines. Consequently, the stock count has become the essential tool to establish and verify the inventory.

Only when people are no longer needed to count and verify stock will the physical stock count disappear. Despite favorable advances in technology, this day still seems many years away.

VI: Notes

1   Kutz, Gregory. *Executive Guide: Best Practice in Achieving Consistent, Accurate Physical Counts of Inventory and Related Property.* Washington: United States General Accounting Office, 2002.

2   See Muller, Max. *Essentials of Inventory Management.* New York: American Management Association, 2003; and Purpura, Phillip P. *Retail Security Shrinkage and Protection.* Boston: Butterworth Heinemann, 1993.

3   Kutz, Gregory.

4   Piasecki, David J. *Inventory Accuracy: People Processes and Technology.* Kenosha: OPS Publishing, 2003, p. 5.

5   Muller, Max; and Piasecki, David.

6   Kutz, Gregory.

7   Uckun, Canan, Karaesmen, Fikri and Savas, Selcuk. Investment in improved inventory accuracy in a decentralized supply chain. *International Journal of Production Economics*, vol. 113, 2008.

Glossary

Term	Like Terms	Description
Adjacencies		A merchandising term referring to the placement of stock and its relative position to other stock. Using market research and sales data, adjacencies are arranged to maximize sales.
APH (average units counted per hour)		APH refers to the rate at which stock is counted during the course of a stock count. It is defined as the total number of units counted (items x quantity) divided by the total time taken.
Asset		Economic resources owned by an enterprise that can be attributed a monetary value. It may include commercial stock, property or equipment.
Asset register	Also known as fixed asset register.	Accounting term referring to an inventory of an enterprise's non-current assets that are primarily held to assist in the production of goods or the rendering of services. These include those that cannot be quickly converted into cash. It may include loaned equipment, buildings, patents, trademarks, software, instance property, plant and equipment.
Auditor		Certified accounting professional whose role is to ensure business and accounting practices are maintained. Responsibilities include verifying that stock counts are completed correctly and that reported stock holdings are accurate.

Barcode	Also known as Global Trade Item Number (GTIM), Universal Product Code (UPC), European Article Number (EAN), Australian Product Number (APN), Manufacturers Part Number (MPN).	A printed representation of text information using a standardized symbology that can be read by a barcode-reading device. The term barcode is commonly used to refer to a unique number in a barcode form printed on goods during manufacture.
Barcode symbology		A two-dimensional representation of text information printed in a standardized array of vertical lines that can be read by a barcode reading device. Some common symbologies are Code 39, EAN-8 and EAN-13.
Counter	Also known as auditor, stocktaker.	Someone who performs a stock count that includes the systematic counting and recording of stock location, item and quantity.
Cut-offs	Also know as period-ends, period-end cut-offs.	The moment in time one accounting period changes to another. Stock deliveries not yet received and included in the perpetual inventory are 'cut-off' and included in the subsequent accounting period.
Cycle stock count		A partial stock count where only a portion of an enterprise's total stock is counted at a time. The cyclic count areas may be based on location, value, category or risk.
Database		Electronic store of data.
Database (inventory)		Logically related collection of files or information in a computer format. Often built on relational concepts, information is arranged using common features or attributes. Databases allow for fast and efficient storage and retrieval of inventory information including item numbers, characteristics and sales data.
Depreciation		Accounting practice where the value of an asset is periodically reduced by an approximate amount which represents the loss of value over its working life.

Distribution inventory system		Integrated computer software and hardware systems that primarily monitor the flow of stock through one or more storage facilities in order to maximize the stock storage space and security; and minimize the duration of stock receiving, storage, picking and dispatch.
Enterprise		Any company, firm or business operating as a commercial institution. This book is concerned primarily with enterprises who maintain, or utilize, inventory information.
Enterprise Information Systems (EIS)	Also known as Enterprise Systems (ES),Enterprise Applications (EA) and Enterprise Resource Planning Systems (ERP).	Large, integrated computer software systems that operate vertically throughout an enterprise. It includes linked software modules such as merchandising stock system, perpetual inventory system and finance and accounting systems. The database is shared by all modules, allowing less repetitive data entry, consistent reporting and greater data access and transparency.
FIFO (first in, first out)		Accounting convention referring to the first (or oldest item price) applied to stock as it is sold.
Fixture		A section or area within a gondola or aisle used to store or display stock.
Floor plan		A visual representation of a retail store's architectural features, including stock fixtures.
Full stock count	Also known as wall-to-wall count.	A complete stock count where all of an enterprise's stock holding is included.
Handheld device	Also known as barcode scanner, portable data terminal (PDT), portable data entry (PDE).	A computer device used to capture data. Typically it includes a barcode scanner, keyboard and screen and is used during a stock count to facilitate the counting and recording of stock.
Heat map		A schematic representation of data where the values of any variable are represented as colours and displayed across a two-dimensional image such as a store floor plan. This allows managers to quickly identify areas of high sales, profits or shrinkage.

Inventory		A noun referring to physical stock, a noun referring to a list of items, or a verb referring to the act of recording items.
Inventory accuracy		The number of items and quantities between two independent inventories that concur. This can be expressed as a percentage of all items or can be calculated by deducting the percentage of errors from 100% (where accuracy = 100% less % of error).
Inventory valuation deviation		Valuation deviation is simply the difference between two inventory stock valuations for the same items. It can be calculated by determining the total valuation for each inventory and deducting one from the other, or it can be calculated by obtaining the valuation difference for each item and summing all differences.
Inventory error		Inventory error is defined as any quantity difference greater than a predetermined tolerance between two counts of the same item in the same location. An item tolerance could be any commercial discrepancy the enterprise deems acceptable. The total number of errors can be expressed as a percentage of the total number of items.
Item		A unique variety of stock usually identified by a unique number such as a barcode, SKU or PLU (see below).
Keypunching	Also known as data entry.	Manually entering data into a handheld or computer without scanning.
LIFO (last in, first out)		Accounting convention referring to the last (or most recent item price) applied to stock as it is sold.
Location (inventory)	Also known as area, section.	An arbitrary area of stock often marked with a unique numbered label to identify the stock. These can be combined with a floor plan to track the progress of an inventory count.
Logistics	See also the related term 'supply chain'.	The systematic planning and implementation of resources necessary to sustain an enterprise; in particular the procurement, distribution and replacement of materials.

Margin	Also known as gross profit, retail margin, profit margin, mark-down.	The sales profit for an item defined as the difference between its cost price and its retail sales price. It is often expressed as a percentage relative to the retail price. For instance, an item bought for $1.00 and sold for $1.50 has a profit margin of $0.50. Expressed as a percentage it has a profit margin or mark-up of 33% ($0.50 ÷ 1.50 x 100). Expressed as a percentage relative to cost, it has a mark-down of 50% (where $0.50 ÷ 1.00 x 100).
Market value	Also known as fair value.	The price an asset would trade in an open, arm's length transaction in a transparent and free market.
Merchandising stock system		Computer software system that manages the arrangement of stock in a retail setting. It draws on sales history, market research and product information and uses floor plans and planograms to visually review and present stock in order to maximize sales.
MRP II (Manufacturing Resource Planning, Mark 2)		Computer software system used by manufacturers that manages and reports the use of raw materials, capital and labour inputs, production scheduling and customer delivery.
Perpetual inventory		Accounting term referring to a continuous item-level inventory record automatically updated as sales, purchases and transfers are made.
Perpetual stock system		Integrated computer hardware and software system that continuously updates, manages and reports a perpetual inventory including purchases, sales, transfers and other stock information in near real-time.
Planogram		Elevation drawing that visually represents stock placement on each fixture. It provides a standing view of the stock, illustrating the placement and adjacencies of each item, allowing for stock to be more easily arranged to maximize sales.

PLU (price look-up code)	Also known as SKU (stockkeeping unit) or part number.	Standardized unique item number used to identify and distinguish a specific type or variety of stock. Commonly in the retail industry PLUs are used at the check-out to record stock as it is sold.
POS (point-of-sale) system	Also known as check-out system.	Integrated computer software and hardware systems that primarily monitor and record the sale of stock and the method of payment in a retail enterprise.
Reinstatement value		The cost to replace an asset with the same or similar asset allowing for any differences in utility, age or obsolescence.
RFID (radio frequency identification)		An electronic device attached to items and used to identify and track them. RFID tags can receive and transmit radio signals. As such they can be detected by readers over a wider range and do not require a direct line of sight, unlike barcode readers.
RGIS™ (Retail Grocery Inventory Services)		The world's largest inventory service provider. Founded in 1958 in Detroit and now in over 25 countries worldwide.
Salvage value		The price an asset would trade in distressed circumstances when there is undue pressure, limited time or unconventional circumstances in which to sell.
Scan		The act of using a handheld scanner to read and record a barcode.
Shrinkage		Stock that is lost, damaged, stolen or spoiled in the course of business. Its cause may be intentional, such as theft by staff, suppliers or customers, or it may result from accidental administrative errors observed in paperwork, receipting, storage, picking or dispatch.
Stock turn		A measure of how quickly an enterprise sells its inventory over a time period. It is calculated by dividing the cost of goods sold by the average inventory. A low stock turnover results from having large stock-on-hand quantities relative to the amount sold, while a high turnover occurs when low levels of stock-on-hand are maintained relative to periodic sales.

Stock		A collective term for items held by an enterprise in the course of business.
Stock count	Also known as physical inventory, physical count, stocktake, stock count.	The act of counting and recording stock in an effort to generate an inventory.
Stock-on-hand		The quantity of stock thought to exist within an enterprise location at a point in time.
Stock sheet		A list or report that itemizes stock details. It is generated or updated in the process of a stock count.
Storplanner™		Merchandising stock system developed by RGIS that utilizes store architectural and inventory information to create visual representations of floor and fixture space.
Supply chain	See also the related term 'logistics'.	The control of materials, information and finances as they move in a process from supplier to manufacturer, wholesaler to retailer.
Tolerance (inventory)		An allowed level of discrepancy between two inventory records of the same item. The tolerance level may be calculated as a percentage of the item's quantity, periodic sales quantity or value.
Validation file	Also known as product master file (PMF), product file, master data file.	An inventory of stock, usually in a computer format, that includes a number of fields such as item number, barcode, description and price. It may be stored on a handheld device and used to verify stock item numbers and details during a stock count.
Valuation		The process of estimating the value of an asset. Depending on the intention of the valuation, the same item might be valued using different valuation concepts and methods.

Index

CPSIA information can be obtained at www.ICGtesting.com
Printed in the USA
LVOW091851220212

269932LV00003B/429/P